The Night Jingles Were Born

The Night Jingles Were Born

WCCO Radio's
Greatest Broadcast Moments

by

Dick Hill

Hill Top Publishing
Edina, Minnesota

ISBN: 978-0-692-47847-9

Hill Top Publishing
Edina, Minnesota

CONTENTS

*This book is dedicated to the memory of WCCO's
Brad Johnson, a world-class broadcaster, and a member of
the Minnesota Broadcasting Hall of Fame. He was as talented
in his new sales career, as he had been in announcing. Brad
believed in relationship selling. He advised prospects to add
8-3-0 to their media mix. They soon became advertisers
and were as excited about WCCO as Brad was.*

ABOUT THE AUTHOR

Minnesota-born Dick Hill is an author and retired advertising executive. He has earned numerous creative, marketing, and broadcast awards. At age 18 he joined WCCO Radio as a pageboy. A wannabe announcer, they let him sharpen his broadcast skills by reading the midnight news over the 50,000 watt clear channel station. Later, he became a decorated Marine Radio Correspondent, covering the Korean War. Hill, a graduate of the University of Minnesota, survived a 35-year advertising career, including 12-years with Campbell Mithun. A media buff, he is an authority on Minnesota broadcasting. Hill lives with his wife, Mary, in Edina, Minnesota.

ACKNOWLEDGEMENTS

A special "Thank You" to all involved, including: Campbell Mithun, General Mills, The Minnesota Historical Society, Pavek Museum of Broadcasting, and WCCO Radio. Also, Dave Lee and Robert Vaughn. And, to my wife, Mary Hill, for her support and patience, while I was writing this book. (It took several years longer than she thought it would.)

FOREWORD

By Dave Lee

Host of "The WCCO Morning News With Dave Lee"

Dick Hill has honored me by asking me to write a foreword for his newest book, ***The Night Jingles Were Born.*** I love the broadcasting business, and jump at the chance to write or talk about it. Especially when it spotlights WCCO's historic milestone – America's first singing commercial. Radio and television is a fascinating subject. And it touches everyone. Its place in a free enterprise society is critically important. It has grown to a multi-billion dollar business and helps support our economy.

Minnesota has a rich history in the broadcast industry, which we can be proud of. WCCO was Minnesota's first radio station with any consistency. Signing on in 1924 with 500 watts, WCCO grew to a powerful 50,000 watt clear channel station, that reaches all of Minnesota's 87 counties, and beyond. And while kilocycles, transmitters, and microphones played a part, it was *people* who made it "Minnesota's Good Neighbor Station." Hill knew, and worked alongside the headliners, Cedric Adams, Bob DeHaven, and Clellan Card. Preserving their history is important to all of us.

Now, a confession. I may be the only living soul that turned down WCCO when asked to audition for the station. I was at KFGO, Fargo, North Dakota, and happy with my job. A few years later, in 1989, when asked again, I joined WCCO. What a wonderful feeling when I entered the WCCO Radio Building on Second Avenue in Minneapolis. It was like joining the major leagues. There to greet me was Roger Erickson, one of the all-star announcers. Before my current early morning slot, Roger showed me the ropes, and how's it done.

Now then, more about ***The Night Jingles Were Born.*** It's an amazing piece of media history. Not everyone knows that WCCO holds the honor for airing the nation's first singing commercial, for *Wheaties.* Dick Hill's pageboy days took place when WCCO dominated its Minneapolis/St. Paul market. And the programming was like an appetizing Minnesota smorgasbord. There were live musical shows with a 20-piece orchestra, cooking and quiz shows. Also, wall-to-wall, play-by–play, sports teams. Including, The Minneapolis Millers, the Minnesota Twins, Vikings, and North Stars. Plus, all the great University of Minnesota Golden Gopher sports teams. (Basketball, football and hockey.)

Over the years, WCCO had its share of disc jockeys - like I once was - and soap operas, like *Oxydol's Own Ma Perkins*. And all those great nighttime shows: *Jack Benny, Amos 'n Andy,* and Frank Sinatra's *Your Hit Parade.* ***The Night Jingles Were Born*** is the WCCO story, and features the station's great moments in broadcasting. Because weather is so important in our region, the book suggests that we're fortunate to have that crackerjack of a weatherman, Mike Lynch. Oh, oh! I hope Mike doesn't see that part. Thanks for listening, good neighbor.

About Dave Lee – For over 20 years, Dave Lee has been the popular host of *The WCCO Morning News with Dave Lee.* He has been nominated as one of the Top Five Major Market hosts, nationwide. He personally has won countless broadcasting awards to help keep WCCO's trophy wall overflowing. An avid sports guy, Dave has done color for Twins games, and currently does play-by-play for the station. For a morning bonus, listeners are enjoying an occasional, "Extra Innings," with Dave Lee and John Hines, at 9:00 a.m.

The Night Jingles Were Born

WCCO Radio's Greatest Broadcast Moments

by

Dick Hill

INTRODUCTION

What? WCCO had disc jockeys? And a live 20-piece orchestra? And more stars than in heaven? Folks can hardly believe what it was like in the 1950s, when nearly every radio was tuned to 8-3-0. WCCO so dominated the Twin Cities market that it followed you wherever you went; the super market, beauty parlor, drug store, bait shop – even the dentist's office. And the radios stayed on until after Cedric Adams delivered his 10 O'Clock Taystee Bread newscast.

I consider myself fortunate to have worked alongside the station's headliners: Cedric Adams, Bob DeHaven, and Clellan Card. They were a way of life with listeners, and made chores a little easier; the day go a little faster. And helped me sharpen my broadcast skills. Long before I joined the station, WCCO made broadcast history by airing the nation's very first singing commercial. A jingle, if you will - *Have You Tried Wheaties?* The historic event took place in the WCCO studios on December 24, 1926. (Christmas Eve.) And successfully I might add, as jingles soon became an integral part of radio, and a successful industry all its own. And it triggered a string of great broadcast moments for WCCO.

The Night Jingles Were Born tells about one of America's great radio stations, WCCO Radio. It's the first book by a pageboy, and offers a new twist on the subject. The pageboy concept was created by CBS on Madison Avenue. It was an image kind of thing. WCCO pages, in their dress blues, by their very presence, were meant to lend style to the station's ambience. And at the same time, lend a helping hand to every department throughout the station.

You young folks, maybe taking a high school, or college media class, will want to devour the book. It's packed with important media history to help you pull higher grades. It tells how WCCO Radio was a media powerhouse for decades. Sadly, but realistically, those days will never return. Today's multi-media choices are too fragmented for any one station to dominate a market like WCCO once did. To fit the times, WCCO reinvented itself into a successful news/talk format station, which it is today.

-1-

MINNESOTA'S BROADCAST PIONEER

Bringing Radio to the Region

"It was like having a theater in the living room."

WCCO didn't invent radio. But the station polished and perfected it, so that many people thought they did. WCCO, AM 8-3-0, serving the key Minneapolis/St. Paul market, wasn't the first station in Minnesota, either. But it's the one remembered, because through the years it has been as much a part of the community as the Land of 10,000 Lakes, the Minnesota State Fair, and the Mall of America. As Minnesota's most important news and information station, WCCO is a modern town crier with its giant 50,000 watt clear channel voice. Minnesota's Good Neighbor Station has been an active part of the community for 90-proud years. Plus, it has become one of America's great radio stations.

WCCO's first milestone was its inaugural broadcast on October 1, 1924. The station dates its history to 1924, but its origin really goes back two more years – to 1922. The real pioneers of radio listening were tuned to WLAG Radio, "The Call of the North." The station was in the Oak Grove Hotel, overlooking Loring Park, in Minneapolis. Its debut, with 500 watts, was at 9:00 a.m. on Labor Day, September 4, 1922. Sadly, WLAG was strapped for money. They struggled with the new medium, and their experiment with radio was short lived. Bankruptcy took place two years later. Donald D. Davis, VP with the Washburn Crosby Company, a firm in the flour milling business, and later known as General Mills, heard of the opportunity to buy WLAG. But first he had to convince his boss, Ford Bell, president, because radio was a losing business. But Bell liked the idea that radio could be a valuable marketing tool in Washburn Crosby's "flour war," with its hometown rival, Pillsbury. (In 2000, General Mills bought Pillsbury, for $10.5 billion, making it the fourth largest food producer in the world.) They acquired the station and went on the air using the WLAG call letters, which were soon to be changed.

The initials of Washburn Crosby Company formed the station's call letters, WCCO. They filed with the bureau of navigation, predecessor to the FCC, in Washington D.C., for the new call letters. Thus, "WCCO" was born. It became known as "The Gold Medal Station." (Clever way to promote their Gold Medal Flour during station breaks.) Crystal sets were set at WCCO-417 meters; radios, that were in short demand, to 8-3-0 kilocycles. WCCO joined the few elite stations around the country that were true broadcast believers. Some early critics said radio would never last.

Here's the modest programming that WCCO offered, as posted by *The Saint Paul Dispatch* on October 2, 1924, the station's second day on the air:

A.M.

9:30	Program for Day
9:40	Weather Report and Market Quotations
10:45	Home Service – Betty Crocker
11:30	Market Quotations

P.M.

1:30	Market Quotations and Weather Report
2:00	Home Service – Betty Crocker
4:00	Message Hour
4:30	Market Quotations
5:30	Children's Hour
6:00	Sports Hour
6:30	Dinner Concert
8:00	Lecture Hour, including Feed Talk
9:00	Weather Report
9:30	Musical Program

Did you notice Betty Crocker's name? The Washburn Crosby Company invented the character in 1921 to personalize letters in response from customers. By 1936, the Washburn Crosby Company had been renamed General Mills, and Betty had become so popular, the company created a face to go along with her signature. In 1950, the first *Betty Crocker Cookbook* was published, and quickly became a staple in American kitchens. Just like a real woman, her image has been updated eight times.

Loud and clear, is how the station came in that first night. To one listener, radio was like having a theater in the living room. Another likened it to a magic moment they'd never forget. Others sent words of thanks for bringing radio to the region. Steadily growing, the station moved in 1925, from the old WLAG site at the Oak Grove Hotel, to new studios on the 12th and 13th floors of the Nicollet Hotel, in downtown Minneapolis. In the same year they opened a 5,000 watts transmitter on the site of an old chicken farm, near Anoka. On that same night, WCCO aired President's Coolidge's inaugural address. In 1939, further expansion became necessary and WCCO moved to its present location in the WCCO Radio Building at 625 Second Avenue South, in downtown Minneapolis.

General Mills had two partners in WCCO's infancy – The Minneapolis Civic and Commerce Association, and the St. Paul Association of Commerce. In 1926 both these civic groups dropped out, and for three years WCCO was the exclusive property of the milling firm. In 1929, a tiny radio network which was just beginning to expand its lines in the Midwest, bought a one-third interest in WCCO. You know that network now as CBS, formerly the Columbia Broadcasting System. William Paley, CBS president, had big plans for the station. With that step, WCCO became a key station in the expanding CBS network. It marked a sharp change for the already growing band of loyal listeners. They'd been accustomed to hearing their favorite WCCO programs on NBC, the National Broadcasting Company. WCCO was part of the first handful of stations to band together in an experiment, to see whether network broadcasting might be possible. There's a statement in an early WCCO prospectus that tells how network broadcasting first came to our area. In 1925, WCCO joined facilities set up by WEAF Radio in New York City, "to establish a single circuit network which will interconnect 18 of the important cities of the United States." (The Minneapolis/St. Paul market ranked 15th.) As broadcasting improved, so did the radios. Motorola, a leading brand, kept making them smaller, a sure sign of improved technology.

The Night Jingles Were Born
Wheaties *made history – and new sales*

Sometime along about 1926, after the birth of a miracle called radio, someone realized that music could sell more than just sheet music, more than just gramophone records. Someone discovered that with the right kinds of music, along with the right kinds of words, radio could sell other things, too. Breakfast food, for instance.

The nation's very first singing commercial – *Wheaties* – was aired over WCCO on December 24, 1926 (Christmas Eve night). And successfully, we might add, as the jingle business soon became a successful industry all its own. And jingles became an integral part of radio. The story behind this landmark event is worth telling. The Washburn Crosby Company, who owned WCCO at the time, had a small problem. Their new brand of whole wheat flakes, launched in 1924, wasn't doing so well. *Wheaties* was plummeting in sales. (The product was competing with Kellogg's well-established brand, *Corn Flakes*.) They knew it wasn't the recipe, or taste. Or, name, for that matter, as "*Wheaties*" was catchy, and seemed to fit. So it had to be something else. Management huddled with WCCO in 1926, when radio was still in its infancy. In the meeting, someone suggested a new kind of commercial. Not a spoken one, but a singing one. A singing commercial, with the right words, or lyrics. So after creating their new commercial, titled, *Have You Tried Wheaties?*, a young male quartet, wearing tuxedos, gathered around a studio grand piano. With their rehearsal behind them, they were ready. There was a festive feel in the air, as it was Christmas Eve. Then the *Wheaties* quartet leaned into the WCCO microphone, and sang these lyrics in perfect harmony:

> *Have you tried Wheaties*
> *They're whole wheat*
> *With all of the bran.*
> *Won't you try Wheaties?*
> *For wheat is the best food of man.*
> *They're crispy and crunchy*

The whole year through. The kiddies never tire of them
And neither will you.
So just try Wheaties,
The best breakfast food in the land.

After the quartet finished, the WCCO Radio audience was stunned. They couldn't believe their ears. They didn't know it at the time, but they had just heard America's very first singing commercial, *Have You Tried Wheaties?* And they liked it. They must have *really* liked it, because one of advertising's best tools, word of mouth, went to work. In the following, days, weeks, and months, sales soared for the soon to become, a favorite breakfast food with families. ("More *Wheaties*, please.") With its jingle, *Wheaties* made a dent in Kellogg's *Corn Flakes*. The novel idea of adding music to a commercial was brilliant. For the melody, a popular tune at the time, *She's A Jazz Baby*, was picked. The lyrics were written by Henry Bellows, station manager, and Earl Gammons, future manager of WCCO. The stunt helped put *Wheaties* on a leading brand path, and created a totally new successful business, the jingle industry.

One year later, in 1927, Washburn Crosby had come up with another smart marketing idea—sports testimonials. *Wheaties* became known as, "Breakfast of Champions." The now famous slogan is attributed to General Mills' ad agency, Knox Reeves, in Minneapolis. Some of the participating sports figures featured on the *Wheaties'* boxes were Lou Gehrig, Jessie Owens, and hundreds more from every sport. Early Minnesota stars included Bronko Nagurski and George Mikan. To commemorate the Minnesota Twins winning the World Series in 1991, Kirby Puckett and Kent Hrbeck, team leaders, appeared on a limited edition of *Wheaties* boxes. I was one of the lucky shoppers able to get one of those *Wheaties* collectables, as they sold out fast at Byerly's, on France Avenue in Edina. Who knows. Maybe if I keep it in mint condition, the Antiques Road Show will appraise it for big bucks.

General Mills was a pioneer in radio programs for kids. *Wheaties* sponsored *Jack Armstrong, All American Boy*, in 1933. Then in 1941, the very first episode of *The Lone Ranger* aired on Mutual, and was sponsored by *Kix*. I was one of the millions of youngsters, glued to the radio, and shouted an occasional, "Hi Ho, Silver." (I was 11 years old, a loyal listener, and liked my *Kix*.)

Meanwhile, that *Wheaties* jingle caused a lot of commotion. Other advertisers wanted in on the new trend. And on and on those singing commercials came – Ivory, Lifebouy, Oscar Mayer – and radio created one of the most potent selling climates known. Advertisers everywhere were putting their messages to music. And whether they knew it or not, they were creating a mood and an image. If reliability, integrity, and absolute quality of product were to be that image, then the musical image must convey that. On and on they came, those singing commercials – Zest Soap, Chesterfields, Jello – becoming almost a part of American culture. They were singable, hummable, and memorable. Each created an image, so that when a listener heard even a few notes, like for J-E-L-L-O, for instance, they were affected by the mood, reminded of the product, and conditioned to buy it.

Dinah Shore, in the late 1950s and early 1960s, sang this theme song on her TV *Dinah Shore Show*. It would have flown off the charts had it been a record:

> *See the USA in your Chevrolet*
> *America is asking you to call.*
> *Drive your Chevrolet through the USA*
> *America's the greatest land of all.*
> *On a highway, or a road along a levee,*
> *Performance is sweeter*
> *Nothing can beat her*
> *Life is completer in a Chevy.*
> *So make a date today to see the USA*
> *And see it in your Chevrolet.*

As a result of Chevy's broadcast campaign, Chevrolet production workers got rich from all the overtime, trying to meet dealer demand. Could it be that General Motors' financial problems started at this very point – from all the hefty wages, benefits, and too much overtime paid out? (GM filed for Chapter 11 reorganization in 2009.)

It's a familiar story now, of how Coca Cola dominated the soft drink field for some 40 years. No one made an in-road into Coke's sovereign domain. But little by little, then a lot by a lot, Pepsi kept chipping away. For 11 years – 1939-1950 – Pepsi used the slogan: "Twice as Much for a Nickel." And Pepsi gained on that cola giant, thanks to this simple jingle:

Pepsi Cola hits the spot,
Twelve full ounces
That's a lot.
Twice as much
For a nickel, too
Pepsi Cola is the drink for you.

And today, while Coke is still on top, Pepsi continues to pour it on, and Pepsi's share of the market is a real concern to the Coca Cola Company. Pepsi hasn't discovered Coca Cola's secret formula yet, but they have made gains in the marketplace. While we're on beverages, another classic advertising jingle that helped move thousands of barrels of beer, is "Land of Sky Blue Waters," for Hamm's Brewery, St. Paul, Minnesota. With its refreshing lake country setting, musical tom-toms and a loveable cartoon bear as the Hamm's mascot, the radio/TV campaign, produced by Campbell Mithun, a Minneapolis ad agency, was the envy of the industry. Here was the jingle:

(Beating tom-toms)
From the Land of Sky Blue Waters,
From the Land of pines' lofty balsms,
Comes the beer refreshing,
Hamm's the beer refreshing.
(Beating tom-toms)
Brewed where nature works her wonders,
Aged for many moons, gently mellowed,
Hamm's the beer refreshing,
Hamm's the beer refreshing,
Hamm's.

And you'll find many other success stories, too, thanks to the singing jingle – "Be Happy, Go Lucky," Chiquita Banana, Go KROGERing. And that's just a few that filled the airwaves. The Kroger Company in Cincinnati did what most other advertisers are afraid to do. They stayed with their jingle slogan for over 50 years. (i.e., Let's Go KROGERing.) Today it's a household word. I recall an announcer in the CNN TV Atlanta studios, being asked about his plans after his shift. "I'm going KROGERing, for one thing," he casually replied to his colleague, while his national and international TV audience learned about his food store preference.

Food chains, including A&P, Safeway, and Kroger, historically poured most of their ad dollars into the print media. In 1960, at the suggestion of Ray Mithun, co-founder of Campbell Mithun, Kroger's open-minded president, Joe Hall, switched a big chunk of newspaper dollars, to radio/TV. And it paid off. Today, Kroger is the #1 food chain, having passed both A&P and Safeway in sales volume. And the jingle, "Let's Go KROGERing," was a driving force behind Kroger's improved sales.

It's fitting that we pay tribute to General Mills for giving us the nation's first singing commercial – *Have You Tried Wheaties?* – which led to the jingle industry. Jingles add an entertainment value to radio that listeners enjoy. And at the same time, for the advertiser, they create a mood and image that the spoken word alone could never do. I'm sure many families will be reminded of *Wheaties* historic achievement, every time they see "Breakfast of Champions" on their kitchen table. I know I will.

We don't know for certain, but I'm pretty sure *they* also sang on that night of America's first singing commercial. Because that's what the Angels of Music do when they're happy. And they were happy for us – the radio listeners – as commercials were going to sound brighter, and be more memorable. We were going to be entertained while we were "being sold." Angels like entertainment, too. And I'm sure they were there – that night jingles were born.

Top Ten Jingles
The author's choices – and maybe yours

1. **Coca Cola** – "I'd Like to Buy the World A Coke"
2. **Oscar Mayer** –"If I Were An Oscar Mayer Weiner"
3. **McDonalds** – "You Deserve A Break Today"
4. **Dr. Pepper** – "Wouldn't You Like to Be A Pepper, Too?"
5. **Chevrolet** –"See the USA In Your Chevrolet"
6. **Hamm's Beer** – "From the Land Of Sky Blue Waters"
7. **Campbell's Soup** – "M'm, M'm, Good"
8. **The Kroger Company** – "Let's Go KROGERing"
9. **Wrigley's Doublemint Gum** – "Double Your Pleasure; Double Your Fun"
10. Honorary – America's first jingle: **General Mills** – "Have You Tried Wheaties?"

Nobody Does It Better
WCCO's trophy wall says it all

Something that has amazed me, WCCO Radio has never lost its enthusiasm for excellence. And that takes in a span of 90 years. Its trophy wall is a true measurement of its achievements. They've won about every broadcast award possible. Including the prestigious Peabody and Marconi trophies for the best station and air personality of the year. Plus, WCCO recently won the National Association of Broadcasters Education Foundation's (NABEF) "Service to America" award, for their year round work on the fight against hunger in Minnesota.

For its service to the community, WCCO is well rewarded with accolades. They continue to receive a host of achievement awards, trophies, thank you letters, letters of commendation, special citations, handwritten appreciation notes, and plaques of all kinds. The station, I know, is appreciative of all its awards collected in its ninety years of broadcasting. If the criteria for "Best Broadcaster," is feedback from the community and industry, the station wins, hands down.

To win those awards, WCCO/CBS management has an innate ability for hiring the right people. Not just the on-air personalities, but for all positions, to keep the station at the forefront of their business. Including the recent hire of Mick Anselmo, WCCO Radio Senior Vice President/Market Manager. He was picked to lead the station to the next level.

If there is one place where the cream rises to the top, it's WCCO. Numerous people have zoomed up the ladder, not only to top positions at the station, but on to CBS in New York, as well. One was Sigfried (Sig) Mickelson. Sig was news director when I first started at the station. He had more irons in the fire than anyone I knew. Sig was in close touch with the people who made the news – the newsmakers. His contacts throughout the community helped develop exclusive stories for the station. His leadership drove the news staff to a higher journalism standard. Two of the newswriters I knew best, were Harry Reasoner and Chuck Sarjeant. Both were top-notch newsmen, and wrote newscasts for Cedric Adams. After a few stops along the way, Reasoner eventually moved on to CBS' *60 Minutes*. Sig was also New York bound. CBS New York, offered him a news director's job in 1950. Mickelson was responsible for America's first TV coverage of the political conventions in

1952. He became president of CBS News from 1954-1961. Ever grateful, he's the one who OKed my reading the news at midnight. Jim Bormann, by the way, took over Sig's old position at WCCO, and did a commendable job. And that's an important point. You don't want the replacement to become just a substitute, or, worse, wear the other guy's shoes. If there's one thing I learned in my 35-year advertising career, it's to wear your own shoes. They're the best fit.

Football, at any level, can be a good training ground for character building. Plus, it can prepare young people for hard knocks in the business world. And when your coach is the legendary Bernie Bierman, well, there's no telling how far you'll go. Phil Lewis would have agreed. His Golden Gopher football experience, under Bernie Bierman's coaching, helped him climb the sales ladder at WCCO. After serving in the Army Air Corps in World War II, Phil joined WCCO as a salesman in 1948. Three years later he was sales manager. His next promotion was the big one – station manager.

Sales always excited me. So, I had many talks with Phil when he was just starting in the sales department. Once, I commented that because of WCCO's huge audience and ratings, it must be an easy sell. I'll never forget his answer. "If that's the case, they wouldn't need salesmen," he said. "The real selling starts after an advertiser signs with us." He went on to explain. "WCCO believes in relationship selling. A big part of my job is maintaining a personal closeness with the ad manager, and his or her advertising agency, and their whole company, when possible. If we ignored our customers after they signed a contract, they would lose interest in their media buy. That's why we start building a genuine, lasting relationship."

The rookie salesman, Phil Lewis, had a good handle on the station's philosophy. His sales lesson stuck with me for a long time. Looking back, I realize the station was ahead of its time with its "win-win" sales concept. (Marketing vs. plain selling.) No wonder Phil Lewis became station manager.

WCCO was a lucky station to have Bob Sutton as program director. His programming skills left an indelible mark on the Golden Age of Local Radio. His claim to fame was *The Saturday Nite Radio Party*. Its classic programs included, *Stairway to Stardom*, and *The Red River Valley Gang*. WCCO's local shows, from the listeners' standpoint, were equal to the network's. No wonder the audience was confused about where the shows originated. But what mattered, they all came through 8-3-0 on the dial, home of WCCO.

Another name that comes to mind regarding excellence, is Bob Woodbury. He was the traffic manager when I started at the station in 1949. At a radio station, "traffic" refers to the scheduling of the paid commercials, public service announcements, and promos, which air every day. Nobody did it better than Bob. As he once explained to me, it helps to be a jigsaw puzzle type of person, to survive in a radio traffic department, as there were lots of pieces to organize and manage. He and his staff were in charge of the station log, which was no easy task to maintain at a station the size of WCCO Radio. He racked up 44 years of service with 8-3-0. The Woodbury name lived on at the station, when his son, Steve, was sales manager a few years after Bob retired.

Perhaps the ultimate compliment about WCCO Radio's excellence, comes from competition. St. Paul's KSTP 1500, knows all about WCCO, and respects their rival Minneapolis broadcaster. One of their announcers was known to say: "You've got it made, if you make it to WCCO."

CBS' Prairie Cash Cow
15th largest market; but first in profits

Please, just because a financial term appears, don't ignore this section. It's essential to the story, and a good history lesson, besides. Nationwide, WCCO was part of an industry with an embarrassment of wealth. From 1942-1944, radio advertising budgets increased from$195 million to $390 million. Radio quickly passed newspapers as a national advertising medium, increasing its share of national dollars from 12% in 1941 to 18% in 1945.

Even the government helped WCCO's phenomenal growth. During World War II, it slapped a 90% excess profits tax on industry to discourage profiteering in war contracts, but allowed excess profits used in advertising taxable at normal rates. Thus, until 1945, sponsors could buy a dollar's worth of advertising on WCCO, and other stations, in effect, for ten cents. Thanks to smart management, top talent, and programming, Minnesota's Good Neighbor Station continued on a roll through the 1960s. As an O&O station, owned and operated by CBS in New York City, WCCO produced more profits, per capita, than its larger counterparts: WBBM Chicago, KNX Los Angeles, and KMOX St. Louis. No wonder the CBS accountants on Madison Avenue called WCCO its "prairie cash cow."

Farm Service Days
WCCO – friend of farm families and Agribusiness

It's been said that Larry Haeg, Sr. did for farm service, in the 1940s and early 1950s, what Sig Mickelson did for news. Haeg, WCCO's first farm director, was a state legislator on the agriculture committee, and operated his own 140 acre farm. Minnesota and western Wisconsin dairy farmers had a special affection for him, and welcomed Haeg to their farms. Broadcasting from their farms, he learned about their operations, and gave them the information they needed to be more productive. With Minnesota's diversified farming, Haeg had plenty of homework in preparing for his broadcasts. Besides dairy practices, he had to be knowledgeable in hogs, sheep, poultry, and all of Minnesota's crops: corn, soybeans, barley, and alfalfa. Haeg's market reports and programs were important to both farmers and Minnesota's Agribusiness, including Cargill, General Mills, Pillsbury, International Multifoods, Land O'Lakes, Minnesota Farmers Union, and The Farm Equipment Association.

When Haeg became general manager in 1952, Maynard Speece carried on Haeg's high tradition of farm service. Then along came Roger Erickson. He was the early morning announcer in the 1960s. As sidekick to Maynard Speece, and future farm directors, he made quite a hit with the farm family. They still remember Roger for his many Farm City Days' broadcasts throughout the state. Roger later joined Charlie Boone to become, perhaps, one of radio's best teams, *Boone and Erickson*. Both are in the Minnesota Broadcasting Hall of Fame, as well as Larry Haeg, Sr.

In the middle 1980s, some family farms were failing. Bankers had encouraged farmers to buy more land and equipment. So they did. Then, the banks foreclosed when the loans failed. A ripple effect hurt main street merchants. Tough times? Yes, but the press made it sound like "the sky was falling" in rural Minnesota. To counteract the doom and gloom, Brad Johnson, WCCO sales, proposed to me a series of five-minute programs, to be broadcast from 15 small towns. (I was VP marketing for the Farm-Oyl Company, St. Paul.) Agri Marketing, a national magazine, ran a cover story on the successful Farm-Oyl Road Show. Incidentally, this was my first return to the station since my pageboy days. It was a new role for me as a WCCO client.

Toward the end of the century, some people – mostly metro folks –

falsely accused WCCO of abandoning the farm market. But the truth of the matter was, that due to the declining farm population – from over 150,000 farms in 1950 to 81,000 today – and with farmers getting more and more information off the internet, and from the university, farm publications, and farm suppliers, WCCO was less needed, in respect to farm data. Thus, along with other large metro stations, WCCO reduced farm service and switched more attention to news, weather, and talk shows. Media historians said it was another sign of the times, and was bound to happen. The station is proud of its contribution to the farm market all these many years, and continues to report farm and Agribusiness news, which is essential to Minnesota's economy.

More Stars Than In Heaven
WCCO and MGM's star systems created legends

During their glory years, both WCCO and MGM used a star system for creating and showcasing top performers. The system was really quite simple: Find, develop, and feature the best personalities possible. And it worked. Both companies were founded in 1924, and were leaders in the entertainment field. Further, both boasted of having "More Stars Than In Heaven." MGM's headliners were Clark Gable, Spencer Tracy, and Wallace Berry. For WCCO it was Cedric Adams, Bob DeHaven and Clellan Card. Sure, Gable had his *Gone With the Wind*, but Cedric had his *Stairway to Stardom*, and the *10 O'Clock Taystee Bread News*, to boot. I've seen both Bob DeHaven and Spencer Tracy perform. They were versatile, and each had lots of loyal fans. For laughs, it was Clellan Card and Wallace Berry. Both were naturally funny. For the best in movies, it's MGM's Dream Factory; for Minnesota radio, WCCO's Good Neighbor Station.

Here is the WCCO Radio on-air family from the 1950s-1960s. See how many legendary voices you may have heard, or heard about:

On-Air Personalities: Cedric Adams, Bob DeHaven, Clellan Card, Larry Haeg, Sr., Maynard Speece, Jim Hill, Darragh Aldrich, Joyce Lamont, Allen Gray, Stew MacPherson, George Grim, Dr. E.W. Ziebarth, Charlie Boone, Roger Erickson, Steve Cannon, Randy Merriman, Franklin Hobbs, Jergen Nash, Dick Chapman

Staff Announcers: Frank Butler, Gordon Eaton, Rolf Hertsgaard, Roger Krupp, Jack Huston, Ed Viehman, Earl Steele, Howard Viken

Sportscasters: Halsey Hall, Herb Carneal, Merle Harmon, Bob Allison, Ray Scott, Dick Enroth, Ray Christensen, Brad Nessler, Marv Conn, Babe LeVoir, Sid Hartman

Musicians: Wally Olson, Ramona (Gerhard) Sutton, Irv Wickner, Biddy Bastien, Dick Link, Willie Peterson, Ernie Garvin, Hal Garvin

Singers: Jeannie (Arland) Peterson, Mary Davies, Sally Foster, Tony Grise, Burt Hanson

Feeding the Network
WCCO wows 'em broadcasting coast-to-coast

William Paley, president of CBS, knew WCCO was capable of big things. So he had his New York network programmers schedule nationwide CBS hookups for its Minneapolis/St. Paul station. The network feeds resulted in good exposure for both the station and Minnesota's 10,000 Lakes. We pageboys got involved, because it meant major assignments, such as greeting and escorting the stars from the airport to the station, and setting up the equipment for the special broadcasts. Some of the celebrities I remember, were: Gene Autry, Edgar Bergen & Charlie McCarthy, Eddie Cantor, Rosemary Clooney, Dennis Morgan, Jimmy Durante, Gary Moore, Arlene Dahl, The McQuire Sisters, The Chordettes, and Mel Torme.

For the most part, the artists from Hollywood and New York had a special affection toward WCCO. But a few thought that our style might be too hokey for them. As one media critic once described the station: "WCCO may be corny, but a very *professional* corny, indeed." Whatever it was, audiences loved the shows on WCCO. And now the rest of the nation was going to be exposed to our style of entertainment. With the network hookups, WCCO, the CBS affiliate for Minneapolis/St. Paul, strengthened its reputation on the national stage.

Gene Autry's "Melody Ranch"
WCCO fans were part of the network broadcast

As a kid, I waited in line to see Gene Autry's action-packed Republic westerns at the Rialto Theater, on Lake Street and Chicago Avenue, in Minneapolis. The best part, there was absolutely no sissy-kissy stuff in any

Gene Autry films. Scratch that. Occasionally, Gene Autry gave a friendly smooch to his pal, Champion, the Wonder Horse. Now, I was going to see him in person during the *Saturday Nite Radio Party*, which I was working as a pageboy. In a national CBS hookup, the station was broadcasting Gene Autry's *Melody Ranch*. All the station personnel were excited, as it was a pretty big deal. We were going coast-to-coast.

It aired in December of 1949 as part of WCCO's 25th Anniversary. Sponsored by Wrigley's Gum, *Melody Ranch* was a popular half hour CBS Saturday night program, usually broadcast from KNX Radio, in Hollywood. WCCO originated the live network show from its 4th floor auditorium studio, in front of 700 excited fans. When Gene Autry opened the program, singing his familiar theme song, *Back In the Saddle Again*, the WCCO live audience instinctively applauded. But no applause was called for in the script. Regardless, it seemed to fit, so there was no big problem. But the Hollywood producer, caught by surprise, looked a little perplexed. (Maybe Minneapolis was on to something, and maybe they'd write some applause into next week's show opening.)

Each episode of *Melody Ranch* had several songs and a story line that kept listeners close to their radio. Gene Autry played himself; Pat Buttram was the comic relief, and sidekick to Gene Autry. (Years later he appeared as Mr. Haney in TV's *Green Acres*, with Eddie Albert and Eva Gabor.) Only a few of the cast members flew in from Hollywood, as fill in actors and musicians were hired locally. Home of the Minneapolis Symphony Orchestra – now Minnesota Orchestra – the Twin Cities were a hotbed for good musicians. The writers knew they'd be broadcasting from Minneapolis, so they took advantage of our Scandinavian setting. Clellan Card auditioned and won the part of a Swede, that got him lots of laughs. As I was distributing the scripts on stage before rehearsal, I noticed that Gene Autry's lines were in a larger font size than the rest of the cast – almost 16 point. Nice trick of the trade for someone's eyes that were fading.

A highlight of the holiday show was hearing Gene Autry's new hit-song, *Rudolph the Red-Nosed Reindeer*. (A two million record seller on Columbia.) It soon became one of the holiday's most popular songs. It is second only to Bing Crosby's *White Christmas*. I'm sure Minnesota's record sales saw a nice blip, as the WCCO fans went for it in a big way.

Eddie Cantor's Faux Pas
Savvy producer knew about the old pressure trick

I had always admired Eddie Cantor, both on the radio for Ipana Toothpaste, and in his Samuel Goldwyn movies. But there was an incident during a Minneapolis Aquatennial broadcast, fed to the CBS network, which changed my mind. Cantor was the star of the musical/variety show being held at the old Minneapolis Auditorium. Cedric Adams was host, with a slew of national and regional acts. Cantor had just finished singing his signature song, *If You Knew Susie*, and received thunderous applause. Out of breath, he entered the control booth that was stage right. Besides Bob Sutton, producer, and an engineer at the control panel, I was also in the booth, on standby, for anything that might come up. Eddie Cantor told Bob Sutton: "Sutton, you're not paying me enough!" The room went quiet. At first we all thought he was joking. Then realized he was dead serious. Eddie Cantor clearly said the wrong thing, at the wrong time, at the wrong place, to the wrong person. Bob Sutton wasn't about to be intimidated. Coming from a circus background, he knew everything about show business, and all the tricks. Sutton, an old pro, wasn't the easy prey Cantor thought he was. Without batting an eye, and without his blood pressure rising one iota, Sutton calmly turned to Cantor and politely reminded him they had a contract, and to get the hell out of the control booth, and get ready for his next number. The words left Eddie Cantor speechless. It was obvious he had never been spoken to before in that manner. He quickly left the control booth, as ordered. Then, Bob Sutton said something that defused the tension that was still hanging in the air: "Must have been that wild applause that stirred him up."

"Quiz of the Twin Cities"
Who's smartest? Minneapolis, or St. Paul?

The rivalry between Minneapolis and St. Paul heated up on Tuesday nights at 7:00 p.m. in the 1940s and 1950s. It was *The Quiz of the Twin Cities*, a zany, but popular local program. This was the same period when national radio quiz shows were in full swing. One was *Doctor I.Q.,* sponsored by Mars Candy, makers of *Milky Way*. What I remember about the program was the saying: "I have a lady in the balcony, Doctor." (The program was broadcast from a theater.)

Quiz of the Twin Cities required two studios; one in Minneapolis, the other in St. Paul. The quizmasters, Bob DeHaven and Clellan Card, had a blast with contestants. And both were masters at goosing the audience for maximum laughter. Here's how the program worked: Each city had a team of three contestants. Each team from both cities answered the same questions. The idea was to see which city – Minneapolis or St. Paul – was the smartest. (A little like TV's *Family Feud*.)

My involvement was on the St. Paul side with Clellan Card, MC, Bill Shepherd, producer, and Harry Larson, engineer. Besides transporting all the broadcast equipment and scripts to WCCO's St. Paul's studios in the historic Hamm Building, I helped with the show. Since the St. Paul contestants could hear their Minneapolis counterpart's answers on the studio speaker, it was my job to closet them during that portion of the show. I had a light rigged up, so Bill Shepherd only had to turn on the switch when it was time for me to bring them back. Then they had their turn at answering the same set of questions. One was: "What's the name of the avenue that runs throughout Minneapolis and St. Paul, and through the University of Minnesota?" Answer: University Avenue. The audience couldn't stop laughing over this one: "What milk do goats like best?"

Before each show on Tuesday nights, the St. Paul crew of *Quiz of the Twin Cities* had a nice meal at the Roman Café in St. Paul. And it was complimentary. Actually, a barter deal, as almost every radio station was into bartering. During the *Man on the Street* program from 5:15-5:30 p.m., broadcast in front of the Golden Rule department store, Clellan Card would mention that a good place to dine in St. Paul was the Roman Café. The plug for the restaurant was in exchange for four, free of charge meals.

Bartering has been around almost from the beginning of time. Today, many Fortune 500 Corporations barter, including St. Paul's 3M Company, on an international basis. As did my grandfather, Thomas Stratton, publisher of *The Miller Sun*, a weekly newspaper in Miller, South Dakota. Times were tough during the Great Depression and farmers couldn't afford frills, or my grandfather's annual subscription fee. But they did raise lots of poultry. So the farmers received *The Miller Sun* every Thursday, and my grandfather was paid in chickens and eggs.

Oh, which city was smartest? I kept tabs during the two years I worked the show. It was almost a dead heat, to give us two smart cities, Minneapolis and St. Paul.

Remembering the Weatherball
"Look! It's red. Warmer weather's ahead."

My wife, Mary, can't believe I really was really up there. I remember it like it was yesterday. It was the turning-on ceremony of the region's tallest advertising icon, the Northwestern National Bank's Weatherball. (Now Wells Fargo.) As a pageboy, I was there, atop the 15-story bank building, helping Bob DeHaven and the WCCO crew, in 1949. As someone pointed out, I may be the only living survivor of this historic event, as I was the youngest participant, only 19 at the time. Which means I may be the only person left to tell the story. So here goes.

The Weatherball was the highest illuminated sign between Chicago and the West Coast. And to officially dedicate it, the bank sponsored a 30-minute program on WCCO Radio at 9:30 p.m., October 7, 1949. Bob DeHaven was the host, with the mayor, Eric Hoyer, bank people and other dignitaries in attendance. An eye-catcher, the huge, round Weatherball was perched above a steel structure some 150 feet tall, mounted on top of the bank building. It was built to withstand winds up to 140 miles an hour. With fireworks and 500 balloons being released, the event had a Fourth of July feel. And some of the lucky people that retrieved a balloon, found a valuable savings account certificate inside.

As always, Bob DeHaven did a bang-up announcing job. Besides welcoming and interviewing the dignitaries, he described the new landmark as the Taj Mahal of weather systems. And he predicted that the community would come to depend on the weather forecasts that could change four times daily. Three sides of the sign flashed "NW" and "BANK," which were clearly visible from miles away. Then the moment the whole town was waiting for – the switching on of the city's new monument, the Bank's Weatherball. All eyes were on the ball atop the sign, awaiting bank president Joseph P. Ringland to throw the switch. Everything went without a hitch when the Weatherball lit up the sky for the very first time. (It was white, for colder.) It become part of the city's skyline for 33 years and flashed different colors to indicate the day's weather forecast. Credit Campbell Mithun, the bank's advertising agency, to come up with a catchy jingle. Here is the Weatherball song, which most everyone knew by heart:

> *When the Weatherball is red,*
> *Warmer weather is ahead.*
> *When the Weatherball is white,*
> *Colder weather is in sight.*
> *When the Weatherball is green,*
> *No change in weather is foreseen.*
> *If colors blink by night or day,*
> *Precipitation's on the way.*

Unfortunately, the Thanksgiving Day fire of 1982 destroyed the Northwestern National Bank Building, and the Weatherball era ended after 33 years of serving the community. The sign was removed and went to the Minnesota Fair grounds in St. Paul, where it stood on display until 2000.

Memorable On-Air Teams
WCCO has a knack for pairing talented people

The movies had their Laurel & Hardy, William Powell & Myrna Loy, and Mickey Rooney & Judy Garland. On radio, WCCO featured these popular teams:

- **Boone & Erickson** -Maybe the best team in radio
- **Howard Viken & Joyce Lamont** – *Dayton's Musical Chimes*
- **Bob DeHaven & Clellan Card** – *Quiz of the Twin Cities*
- **Ramona Gerhard & Burt Hanson** – Organist/singer
- **Herb Carneal & Halsey Hall** – Twins baseball
- **Steve Cannon & Morgan Mundane** and all the Little Cannons
- **Sid Hartman & Dave Mona** – *Sports Huddle**
- **Chad Hartman & Sid Hartman** – *Chad Hartman Show**
- **Dave Lee & John Hines** – *Extra Innings**

* Still on the air

Ohhh! Those Golden Voices
WCCO's staff announcers were crème de la creme

They were the utility players of radio. They could play many positions, and mastered them all. There were eight of them. Each with perfect diction and blessed with great announcing skills, so listeners seldom heard a flub. These, Jack-of-all-trades, gave station breaks, delivered commercials, presented the news, and performed as program announcers and disc jockeys. And, as required in radio, they could ad lib with the best of them.

I've just described the WCCO cadre of staff announcers, who played a major role in the station's Golden Age of Local Radio. Their voices were a dead giveaway to which station you had on – WCCO, of course. Their rich, deep, golden, articulate voices became a trademark of WCCO. I admired them all: Frank Butler, Gordon Eaton, Rolf Hertsgaard, Roger Krupp, Ed Viehman, Jack Huston, Earl Steele, and Howard Viken. Howard was the rookie and joined the station a little after I did, in 1950, coming from KDAL AM, Duluth, Minnesota. A former U.S. Marine, Howard served in Iwo Jima during one of the bloodiest battles in World War II history. His combat training would come in handy when cutting across Second Avenue, in front of the station. It was a doozy to cross.

Howard Viken was surrounded by some of the best in the business. In no time he would pick up valuable pointers and tricks of the trade. Bob Sutton, who hired him, said the listeners were "gonna love this guy." I vividly remember him delivering his first commercial on WCCO for Land O'Lakes Ice Cream. He made you want to buy some. The whole station was impressed. It didn't take a psychic to predict that Howard Viken would become a major player on Minnesota's Good Neighbor Station. From that first day, he was on his way to an illustrious 39-year career with WCCO. Listeners did indeed "love him," as the program director predicted. Today, Howard Viken is one of the station's legendary voices, and was inducted into the Minnesota Broadcasting Hall of Fame in 2004.

While Howard was getting settled in his new job, his colleague, Frank Butler, was contemplating a change. The move was a few years away, as Frank had a goal and a plan. Confident of his talent, he left the station in 1961 for freelance work in Hollywood. Considered the most competitive announcing market, he scored big on his audition. Frank won the voice over job on the *Dick Van Dyke Show*, that ran for five-years, often as the number one TV show. It showed the kind of talent WCCO had hidden in Minneapolis/ St. Paul.

Competition wondered where WCCO found all their talented people. Actually, some of the talent found WCCO. Bob Sutton, former program director, told me that he averaged five audition tapes each week. Radio people from all over the country wanted to be on WCCO's roster. Whereas on-air personalities are usually hired for personality first, and voice second, staff announcers were hired for their amazing voices and announcing skills. Often, they had to perform network cut-ins. Maybe a CBS newscast was airing a commercial not germane to the Twin Cities; and/or maybe the sponsor didn't buy this market. Howard Viken, for example, with earphones, had to listen to the network announcer read his spiel, while he was "cutting in" with a local commercial or announcement. Not easy. Howard had to be in sync with the network announcer, and end his spot precisely at the same time. It required discipline and concentration. It was a good learning experience for me, as I had to do the same thing at WBIZ, Eau Claire, Wisconsin, a year later, with the Mutual Network. Thank goodness you were allowed a few mistakes on 250-watt stations.

Many announcers jump ship when they receive an offer from a larger market. (Minneapolis/St. Paul ranks 15th.) But most of the WCCO announcers were content to stay put. (Big fish in the little pond, theory.) Who needed Chicago, St. Louis, Kansas City, or New York, when you were already with a blue chip station?

Greatest Broadcast Moments
WCCO Radio through the years

Recreating history is a wonderful thing for the generations that didn't live it. And one good source for historical stories is WCCO Radio. The station has aired thousands of them during its 90 years in broadcasting. Here are 25 headlines from its archives; many are milestones, as noted:

- ***WCCO Radio's inaugural broadcast** – October 1, 1924
- ***America's first singing commercial – "Wheaties"** – 1926
- **Cedric Adams' first news broadcast** – 1934

- **"Stairway to Stardom" premiers** – 1939
- **Japan bombs Pearl Harbor** – December 7, 1941
- **Bruce Smith, Gopher All American, wins Heisman Trophy** – 1941
- **Minnesotans celebrate end of World War II** – September 2, 1945
- **"Bernie Bierman Football Show" premiers** – 1946
- ***WCCO celebrates 25th Anniversary** – 1949
- **National broadcast of Gene Autry's "Melody Ranch"** – 1949
- **Weatherball turning on ceremony** – October 7, 1949
- **Howard Viken delivers his first WCCO commercial** – 1950
- ***Quiz of the Twin Cities celebrates 100th program** – 1950
- **Bob Hope stars on Aquatennial broadcast** – 1951
- **Cedric Adams, Minnesota's first radio superstar, dies** – 1961
- **Golden Gophers win Rose Bowl** – 1962
- **Boone & Erickson score first interview with Senator Hubert H. Humphrey, nominee for Vice President** – 1964
- ***WCCO celebrates 50th Anniversary** – 1974
- **United States Bicentennial Celebration** – July 4, 1976
- **Twins win World Series** – 1987
- **Farm City Days, Kasson** – 1988
- **150 Years of Statehood Celebration** – 2008
- **Dave Lee's Gutter Bowl 7; Tournament benefits military families** – 2013
- ***WCCO Radio Station of the Year** – 2013
- ***WCCO celebrates 90th Anniversary** – 2014

*Milestones

Radio Testimonials
We tend to buy from those we know and trust

WCCO Radio leads in the use of testimonials in Minnesota broadcasting. Advertisers learned that if they used a popular spokesperson, like Dave Lee, for instance, the commercial would get greater attention, vs. using an anonymous voice. (Dave's signature sponsors include Country Hearth Breads, Federated Insurance, Kinetico Water Systems, and Walser

Automotive.) That's why many WCCO advertisers are smartly turning to testimonials. I'm hearing more and more of them, on WCCO, given by: Dave Lee, John Williams, John Hines, Mike Lynch, Mike Max, Denny Long, Al Malmberg, and Jordana Green. Each has his/her own delivery style. Each denotes believability and trust. Listening to them makes me want to buy, the true test of any commercial. As in most sales situations, we tend to buy from those we know and trust.

Station Breaks
Some were like mini-programs

The FCC (Federal Communications Commission), requires radio stations to identify themselves on the hour and half hour. Most listeners take station breaks for granted, and barely hear them. (Unless they're traveling by auto/truck and want to know what town/station they're listening to.) When I worked at WCCO in the 1950s, the station ID's were live and in a 30-second format of three parts. First, the station ID (call letters), then a 15-second commercial, followed by the time and temperature. They often started with a cue from the network on the hour or half hour. (Actually, at 29:30 or 59:30 to allow for the 30-second break.) The network cue was: "This is the Columbia Broadcasting System."* Then, the local WCCO announcer, i.e., Frank Butler, would come in with: "This is WCCO Radio, with studios in Minneapolis and St. Paul." Next, Frank would read his 15-second spot. That done, checking the clock, he would give the time and temperature. If still some seconds to spare, he would fill with a program promo, or, weather. It was always done very businesslike. Then, straight up on the hour, it was back to the network, or maybe on to a local program.

Bob Sutton, program director, and always the innovator, wanted some variety in station breaks. He broke the tradition of using one announcer by squeezing three voices into the break preceding the 7:00 a.m. *CBS World News Roundup*. Howard Viken gave the station ID, Frank Butler delivered the fifteen-second commercial, and Jack Huston gave time and temperature. All live, all without miscues. It worked. The voice variance in that short time span caught your attention. More than an ordinary station break, it was like a mini-program. Sutton's premise was that since WCCO had all these great voices, why not use them. He didn't use the three voice format every time, but just often enough to break the routine. And to my knowledge, it was exclusive to WCCO.

One early Sunday morning I was on switchboard duty when I heard Roger Krupp give a station break over the lobby monitor. There was nothing unusual about that. Except that what did catch my attention was the unusual way he gave the temperature, on that cold, crisp, December morning. Instead of reporting, "zero degrees," he ad libbed the word "nothing." (What? The temperature was "nothing?") Today, it's no big deal. But in 1950, station breaks were sacred. It was like, heaven-forbid, Roger Krupp had burped in Church. A few days later he was reprimanded for his little on-air joke. But the scolding couldn't have been too severe, as Roger Krupp was an industry legend. At NBC in New York, he was the youngest network announcer in radio – only 18. During his nearly 20 years with NBC, he appeared on hundreds of programs and soap operas. Now, in the prime of his life, and heading toward retirement, he was a staff announcer on WCCO. A good one, even when he was on a creative binge with his station breaks.

*In 1974 CBS dropped the Columbia Broadcasting System name, and became CBS.

Minnesota's Good Neighbor
WCCO lives up to its slogan

A good slogan can go a long way in promoting a product, or company. One that comes to mind is, "Never Stop Improving," for Lowes Home Improvement Stores. Another, WCCO's "Minnesota's Good Neighbor." Used now for more years than anyone can remember, the slogan is burned in our minds for an effective piece of advertising. And it rings true. WCCO Radio has been an active "partner," to the community, all during its 90 years in broadcasting.

Honoring Minnesota's Good Neighbors has been a tradition on WCCO for decades. Every morning, just before eight o'clock, Dave Lee announces the Good Neighbor of the Day. Popp Communications, active in helping our military and their families, is the sponsor for this "tip of the hat" to our volunteers. Incidentally, did you know that Minnesota ranks high in the nation for volunteer work and donations? Good neighboring is part of our makeup. It takes after our "Minnesota Nice," reputation.

Minnesota Broadcasting Hall of Fame
Only the best-of-the-best achieve this award

In any profession, special recognition is a goal most people strive for. WCCO Radio has an outstanding record in this endeavor. They have more inductees in the Pavek Museum of Broadcasting's Minnesota Broadcasting Hall of Fame, than any other regional radio station, or related industry. Here are the 35 WCCO Radio honorees who have won the prestigious award. See how many names you identify with, or have heard about:

Cedric Adams – Minnesota's first radio superstar
Mick Anselmo – Current General Manager
Charlie Boone – "Boone & Erickson Show"
Steve Cannon – On-air personality
Clellan Card – On-air personality
Herb Carneal – Twins announcer
Ray Christensen – Sportscaster
Mary Davies – Singer
Bob DeHaven – On-air personality
Roger Erickson – "Boone & Erickson Show"
Eric Eskola – Newscaster
Bob Fransen – Newswriter
John Gordon – Twins announcer
Allen Gray – "Housewives Protective League"
Larry Haeg, Sr. – General Manager
Halsey Hall – Twins announcer
Sid Hartman – Sportscaster
Franklin Hobbs – "Hobbs House"
Arv Johnson – Newscaster
Brad Johnson – Sales account executive
Clayt Kaufman – General Manager
Kim (Jeffries) Kotola – On-air personality
Joyce Lamont – On-air personality
Phil Lewis – General Manager
Randy Merriman – On-air personality
Brad Nessler – Sportscaster
Jeanne (Arland) Peterson – Singer/pianist
Eleanor (Mondale) Poling – On-air personality
Robert B. Ridder – Management
Ray Scott – Vikings announcer

> **Al Shaver** – North Stars hockey announcer
> **Don Shelby** – On-air personality
> **Howard Viken** – On-air personality
> **Roger Kent Vogel** – Newscaster
> **Steve Woodbury** – Sales Manager

The Minnesota Broadcasting Hall of Fame is an award anyone in the industry would love to receive.

Commercial Champion
Counting 90 years of commercials

Some media buyers wanted to do something special for WCCO's 90th Anniversary. Not content with just mailing a congratulatory card, they did something that radio buffs would be interested in. Fast with figures, they thought it would be a lark to tally all the commercials heard over WCCO Radio, during its 90 years in broadcasting. So, getting out their calculators, they went to work and started crunching the numbers. They estimated the number of commercials given during its nine decades of broadcasting. The 90-year grand total they came up with, was – are you ready for this – **8,278,200 commercials**. (That's unofficial, of course.)

What a coincidence. A good friend of mine, and a loyal listener of WCCO Radio, said he thought he heard that many yesterday. (Pun intended.)

90th Anniversary Award
WCCO Radio joins list of Minnesota's Wonders

In an earlier book, *Hooked on Minnesota*, I selected Minnesota's great wonders. There were ten of them; many are natural, some man-made; all contributing to Minnesota's good life. In honor of their 90-years of service to the community, I'm adding WCCO Radio, Minnesota's Good Neighbor Station, as the 11th honoree.

Minnesota's Great Wonders

10,000Lakes
Mall of America
Boundary Waters
Mayo Clinic
Minnesota State Fair
Paul Bunyan
Voyageurs National Park
Minnesota Casinos
Mississippi Headwaters
University of Minnesota
WCCO Radio

We Minnesotans are a lucky bunch to have so many great attractions for ourselves, and for visitors. Check the list. How many of the above "Wonders" are you acquainted with, or have experienced? ∎

-2-

THE CEDRIC ADAMS PHENOMENON

Minnesota's First Superstar

Fans loved Cedric Adams because he was one of them

Just as Babe Ruth "built" Yankee Stadium, Cedric Adams helped create one of the nation's leading radio stations. For 30 years he was the best-known radio personality in the Midwest. He was the home run hitter for WCCO Radio, serving the key Minneapolis/St. Paul market. No local or regional personality has ever matched his tremendous popularity – or ratings. Today, we call those Cedric Adams years – the 1930s-1950s – The Golden Age of Local Radio. Folksy, with a warm and friendly, deep authoritative voice, he was a media icon. Adams was Minnesota's first radio superstar. Men and women dropped everything to catch his newscasts. The first was at 12:30 p.m., and followed *Oxydol's Own Ma Perkins,* the popular soap opera, giving him a huge lead-in audience.

Born in Adrian, Minnesota, Adams attended the University of Minnesota. His media career started as a reporter in the 1930s for *The Shopping News,* a free shopper in south Minneapolis, where I lived. He graduated to the *Minneapolis Journal,* and soon became a featured daily columnist. ("In This Corner," with Cedric Adams.) He was an advocate of many causes, including the banning of firecrackers that maimed dozens of Minnesotans every 4th of July holiday. By the time he added radio to his schedule, he was an accomplished journalist, and the #1 columnist in the *Journal*.

His first newscast was on WCCO Radio in 1934. He soon caught the attention of listeners and advertisers. The public had never heard anyone quite like him. He had one the most recognizable voices in radio. Just a few words and you knew it was Cedric. Sponsors loved him, because he was a natural salesman on the air. His signature advertisers were Taystee Bread, Twin City Federal, (now TCF), McGarvey Coffee, Peters Meats and Phillips 66 (Phillips Petroleum). All were enamored with Cedric, as their products/service "sold like hotcakes." And there was a waiting line to have him as a spokesman.

Not many of us would be able to handle all the attention and success that Cedric Adams achieved. He had a healthy absence of ego. No prima donna, he welcomed his fans like old friends, and wanted to hear what they were thinking. "If I ever stop knowing people, and what they think, I'm through," he often told interviewers. Dr. Ralph G. Nichols, of the University of Minnesota, said this about Adams: "Cedric always assumed his listeners wanted to hear what he had to say – he used his voice to reveal his own emotional reaction to the news – he revealed his humanness by making errors and admitting them." (Once on the air he admitted having a slight drinking problem.)

No other local broadcaster has ever dominated a market like Cedric Adams. Or, even come close. His dual media role – print and broadcast – gave him tremendous exposure, and heightened his popularity. His whirlwind work schedule consisted of writing a daily column, broadcasting two daily newscasts, sponsor conferences, production meetings, and civic and press functions that today's paparazzi would have loved to cover. On the go throughout our region, Adams made some 120 personal appearances each year. Many of them with the *Cedric Adams Open House Road Show*, playing in school auditoriums and gymnasiums all over the region. A typical day started at his office at the *Minneapolis Journal* where he wrote his daily column. Then he went to the WCCO studios for his *Noontime News* at 12:30 p.m. After the broadcast, and some chitchat with colleagues, it was up to his office on the fourth floor of the WCCO Radio Building. Here he did correspondence, worked the phones, and planned out the rest of his day. (Which ended at 10:15 p.m., after his last newscast.)

I often saw Cedric arrive at studio "A," sometimes minutes before going on the air with his *Noontime News*. There was no time to check the news copy, much less scan it, as all announcers are trained to do. He just plunged into the newscast when the red light came on. He trusted his writers, such as Harry Reasoner and Chuck Sarjeant, to write the copy in his style, and make it easy to read. And yes, there were times when he stumbled on some of the foreign names or places. But he just gave his famous infectious laugh, and everything was forgiven with his loyal listeners. The public loved his down-to-earth style, and expected a few bloopers when Cedric was on the air. After all, Cedric was one of them.

One time, outside the same studio, there was an incident that taught me something about personal agendas. It was five minutes before airtime, and no Cedric. Bob Sutton, program director, started to worry. He instructed Ed Viehman, a staff announcer, to standby in case Cedric didn't show for his noontime newscast. Ed, who substituted for Adams, would receive a talent fee for reading Cedric's news. I heard Ed say: "OK, I'll stand by. But if I do, then I should get paid my fee, whether he shows or not." In fairness to Viehman, I know he did have to wait around plenty of times. Then, at the last minute, Cedric would appear, and, of course, no fee for Viehman. At the time, I felt that he wasn't being a good team player; that he had his own agenda. But now, looking back, I believe Ed was just trying to make a point. (Good for him.) As it turned out, Ed subbed for Cedric that day, and was paid for his performance. As always, he did an admirable job of reporting the news. After leaving the station in the late 1950s, Ed Viehman turned to politics and was made the State Republican Party Chairman.

The rules were different for Cedric, and his fans knew it. His million-dollar laugh made him the most popular broadcaster in the Twin Cities. His bloopers became his trademark. After landing the prime 10 O'Clock Taystee Bread news slot, his popularity soared like a rock star. And like that rock star, his entourage was always close by during his 10-12 hour days. His staff included assistants, producers, five secretaries (mostly for his fan mail), and a full time chauffeur.

This story about Cedric has been told many times. And it's true. Families wouldn't go to bed until hearing his last broadcast of the day. According to Northwest Airlines pilots flying into the old Wold Chamberlain Field airport, the Twin Cities went "dark" immediately following his 10 O'Clock Taystee Bread News. Cedric's signoff was the listeners' cue to call it a day.

"Stairway to Stardom"
Amateurs that made the cut, showed their stuff

Radio was the perfect platform for amateur musicians. Nationally, listeners tuned in by the millions and cheered for their favorites. One act – The Hoboken Four – featured Frank Sinatra on the Major Bowes *Original Amateur Hour,* on NBC. The skinny, but talented kid, fronted the group in 1935, and pulled off a win. He soon left the group to sharpen his singing style with two of the hottest bands in the business – Harry James and Tommy Dorsey. Then, wanting to do it "his way," he went solo. In no time he was on top of the heap in the city that never sleeps – New York. Meanwhile, in Minneapolis, WCCO was creating its own amateur show. Like Sinatra, WCCO also aimed for the stars, and launched *Stairway to Stardom.* From the first broadcast in 1939, it was a runaway hit. Cedric Adams, as host, made history with the rating system. His *Stairway to Stardom* program had the highest Hooper rating of any local radio show in the nation. (Hooper preceded the Nielson and Arbitron rating systems.) *Stairway* provided an opportunity for amateurs of all ages to show their stuff. And if they won, it could catapult them to the next level – a spot on the *Cedric Adams Open House Road Show.* Once a month the troupe visited towns all over WCCO's listening area, usually broadcasting from school auditoriums or gymnasiums. A few of them – the lucky few – pursued a professional musical career.

Cedric Adams was the perfect host. He made his contestants feel right at home, nudging them to perform like pros. The show featured singers, pianists, organists, guitarists, violinists, harmonicists, and accordionists. Once there was an older fellow playing a sweet potato instrument. He didn't win, but the audience enjoyed his novelty act. One contestant, a 15 or 16-year old girl from southern Minnesota, had a big booming voice. Today, I'd say she sounded similar to Brenda Lee. She stole the show that night, and was one happy gal. Another happy winner was Mary Davies, who went on to be a featured singer at the station. Years later, she played Carmen the nurse in Clellan Card's *Axel and His Dog,* on WCCO TV. Both she and Clellan Card are in the Minnesota Broadcasting Hall of Fame.

Stairway didn't have judges. Instead, an audience applause meter was used. The more applause for your act, the better chance you had of winning. In the fall and winter, the program aired weekly from the station's auditorium. In the summer, it went outdoors. It was broadcast live from the beautiful shores of Lake Minnetonka, just twenty miles west of downtown Minneapolis. Ahead of its time, *Stairway to Stardom* was a forerunner to FOX's *American Idol*.

Cedric's Big Payday
Pageboys knew everyone's worth

Quite by accident, I had an occasion to see Cedric Adams' paycheck while working in the WCCO mailroom. (The envelope wasn't sealed properly.) It wouldn't be proper to reveal the numbers, but I can say this. Cedric was certainly Minnesota's highest paid entertainer. While the rest of his colleagues were earning hundreds, Cedric Adams was paid thousands. (And worth every penny.) Like a double agent, I quickly put the check back in the envelope, and resealed it with Scotch Brand Tape so no one else would see what I saw. Until now, I've never told a soul about the incident. You're the first to be in on this little secret.

Getting the News to Cedric
The news had to follow Cedric on remotes

Frequently, I read the 10 O'clock Taystee Bread news before Cedric Adams did. But it's not as it sounds. *The Cedric Adams Open House Road Show* travelled monthly to towns in the station's listening area, and made quite a hit with the rural audiences. Prior to Cedric's evening newscast – which was the highlight of the event – he and his troupe would perform a live 90- minute show, held mostly in school auditoriums or gymnasiums. Many of the performers were the winners from his *Stairway to Stardom* program. When broadcasting from Appleton, Minnesota, for example, at about 9:00 p.m. I started reading Cedric's news copy by phone from the announcer's booth in the newsroom, to his secretary, Marilyn. An expert typist, she typed it out in script style at the broadcast site. (No Fax or Email in those days.) The news staff didn't care for these remotes, because once the news was phoned in, there was little chance of Cedric giving any breaking news, like he could from the home studio. With just seconds before airtime, Cedric would scan the news copy that had been called in minutes before. He didn't have time to thoroughly check the copy for typos or unfamiliar words. Thus, an occasional blooper occurred. But no worry. Cedric's infectious laugh would follow, and his fans would laugh with him. That was Cedric Adams.

I was working in Campbell Mithun's Chicago office when I heard the news that Cedric had passed away on February 18, 1961. His family, WCCO Radio, the broadcasting industry, and his thousands of fans, were in shock. Cedric was only 58. Dwight Reynolds, one of my colleagues, said I was sure lucky. He went on to say that most people had only heard him on radio, or seen him on TV, whereas I watched him work – and got to know him during my pageboy days. Everyone at the station looked up to Cedric Adams. Including me, while a wannabe announcer. He was the greatest.   ■

- 3 -

WHEN PAGEBOYS "RAN" WCCO
Underfoot and Underpaid
Pageboys were eager to learn; anxious to help

Like the dinosaurs, WCCO pageboys are gone, but not forgotten. Their mystique lives on through the pages of this book, as I was a pageboy, I'm proud to say, for nearly two years. CBS, on Madison Avenue, New York City, came up with the pageboy concept. It was an image kind of thing. WCCO pages in their dress blues, by their very presence, were meant to lend style to the station's ambience. And, at the same time, lend a helping hand to all departments throughout the station. Similar to interns, we were college students, and worked part time. I was the fifth member of the pageboy staff in 1949. The others were John Bowles, Paul Protengier, Don Swanberg, and George Wilson. Robert Vaughn joined us in 1950, and tells about his experiences later in this section.

How's this for a job description: Office boy, tour guide, usher, studio set-up helper, chauffeur, VIP escort, switchboard operator, and station gofer. With our multifaceted duties, you might say we "ran" the station – from the bottom up. The McJob level pay didn't bother me, as the opportunity was awesome. They even let me read the midnight news on the 50,000 watt clear channel station.

You couldn't apply for a pageboy position from off the street. Instead, you had to be recommended, as at West Point or the Naval Academy. My sponsor was Brown Radio Institute in Minneapolis, now Brown College in Mendota Heights, Minnesota. I was a student there in 1949 when Richard (Brownie) Brown, the owner, asked if I wanted to work at WCCO, as a page position had opened up. Would I! What wannabe radio announcer wouldn't. Some advice Brownie gave me before I went for my interview: "There is no better training ground than WCCO Radio for an aspiring young announcer. If you get the job, you'll be surrounded by top-notch mentors. So, keep your eyes and ears open, and learn the biz. End of sermon."

With those words of wisdom, I took off for the station. After a few wrong turns, I finally found the WCCO Radio Building on Second Avenue South, smack in downtown Minneapolis. Knowing they operated by the clock, I made sure I was on time for my interview. Stepping off the elevator on the second floor, I was hit by a bright blue wall in the lobby. The lobby monitor was broadcasting a live musical program. Martha Olson, receptionist, warmly greeted me and chatted with me like I was an old friend. (The same nice lady that would show me how to run the switchboard a week later.) People were whizzing past me with their yellow legal pads, clipboards and coffee. Some had stopwatches. It was obvious they were preoccupied, because all they could spare me was a quick smile. But I didn't mind. This was radio. And I wanted to be part of it.

Mr. Jack Lucas, personnel manager and pageboy supervisor, was very professional, and thirtyish. He invited me to sit while he studied some papers. (Maybe about me.) This was my big moment. After a 30-minute interview I was hired. From that moment on he was "Jack." No more "Mr. Lucas." (That's how radio people were – cool.) The pay was $30.00 a week for the 40 hours that I planned to work, while attending radio school, then later, college. For a kid of 18 who wanted to break into radio, WCCO was a neat place to start. It was the dominant station serving the Minneapolis/St. Paul market, and was owned and operated by the Columbia Broadcasting System (now CBS). The timing was perfect. I joined the station during its 25th Anniversary, when nearly all the radios were tuned to WCCO. (The station had a whopping 70% share of market.) Lots of Hollywood and CBS radio stars came to Minneapolis for the broadcasting milestone, resulting in overtime for the pageboys, and lots of special programs for the listeners.

Pages worked in every nook and cranny of the station, and knew everyone. (There were over 100 employees in 1949.) We were eager to learn, and anxious to help. Even though I could barely spell it, we had an esprit de corps attitude that pulled us together. In our rush to do a good job, we were often underfoot. But no matter, the WCCO staff was quick to forgive.

In between assignments I was guilty of hanging out with the announcers. Often I was found in the announcer's booth with Frank Butler, Gordon Eaton, or Howard Viken, or, whoever was on duty. I liked watching them give station breaks and read commercials. Frank Butler taught me a lot. He was flawless. Never rushed, he romanced every word. Gordon Eaton was gifted with golden tones that the female listeners swooned over. Howard Viken was the epitome of a Midwest announcer. He had the voice and the style that made him stand out. I learned a lot from all my mentors. But it was a "no-no" to bother the announcers. Luckily, it seemed that we pageboys had Diplomatic immunity, so I got by with it.

We worked closely with the program department. Bob McKinsey, assistant program director, had us print and organize scripts for the 50+ live programs each week. First, we ran off 15 copies of each program on the mimeograph/ditto machine. (Not like today's Xerox speed machines. These babies you had to crank by hand) Each set of scripts ran about 20 pages. Then we collated and distributed them to the respective departments (i.e., program, traffic, promotion, engineering, continuity, and to the participating talent). It took longer than it should have, as we scanned the scripts as we worked on them. Just one glance told you the station had some pretty good writers. Including, Joyce Lamont. Before she became talent, she was a copywriter on the continuity staff. We pageboys gave her scripts high marks, especially for *Quiz of the Twin Cities*, a program I was involved with on Tuesday nights, my favorite assignment.

Dress Code
Dress blues added swagger to parading pageboys

There was a dress code for pageboys. We wore a dark blue uniform that matched the WCCO/CBS studio décor. Our blue slacks had an eye-catching gold stripe. The jacket had shiny gold buttons that caught everyone's eye.

We set it off with a starched white shirt and dark blue tie. My new uniform was off the rack, but had a tailor fit. (I had to wait one day to have it altered and customized.) WCCO didn't skimp. For accessories, I took home three Arrow white shirts, a blue tie and a pair of black Florsheim shoes, size 10 ½, with four pairs of sox to match. The tailor told me my 29-inch waist size was the smallest he'd seen among the pageboys. (I didn't fill out until a few years later in the Marine Corps.) We weren't required to wear the jacket while working around the office, or when setting up the studios for broadcast. Our full uniform was saved for the public. As we paraded down the hallway in our dress blues, some WCCOer's thought they detected a slight swagger – a little like the U.S. Marines. As one of the announcers used to say: "You pageboys sure add class to the joint."

The Wannabe Announcer
Broadcasting was the author's career goal

No one wanted to be a radio announcer more than I did. I caught the radio bug from listening to all those great network programs in the 1940s and 1950s: *Fibber McGee & Molly, Amos 'n Andy, Jack Benny, Charlie McCarthy*, and my mother's favorite soap opera, *Ma Perkins*. I especially liked the commercials, and the announcers who delivered them. One was Don Wilson, for *Jello*, on the *Jack Benny Show*. Another, Harlow Wilcox, was spokesman for Johnson's Wax on *Fibber McGee and Molly*. Ken Carpenter, announcer for Bing Crosby's *Kraft Music Hall*, also stood out. As did the brothers, Ken and Wendell Niles.

Early on, advertisers discovered that radio was a personal way to get to the minds of people. The human voice influenced listeners and sold products like hotcakes. And I wanted to be part of this hot, growing industry. At about age ten I used my mom's big cooking spoon as a microphone, and pretended to be a big-time CBS network announcer. By age 15, I was really into it. I had saved my allowance and bought a new Webcor Wire Recorder. On the first day I interviewed nearly everyone in the neighborhood. The next day I knew I wanted to go to radio school. I sent away for a free brochure from Brown Radio Institute on East Lake Street in Minneapolis. The school guaranteed an announcing job after their six-month course. I enrolled after high school and got the surprise of my life about one month into schooling. Richard (Brownie) Brown recommended me for a pageboy position at WCCO Radio. The moon must have been just right, because I got the job. It was the first step toward a 35 year broadcasting and advertising career.

Reading the Midnight News
A rare opportunity for a wannabe announcer

Never in my wildest dreams did I think I'd be giving the midnight news over WCCO. Dr. E. W. Ziebarth, news analyst and my speech instructor at the University of Minnesota, suggested the idea to Sig Mickelson, news director. It wasn't in prime time, so I'm sure management thought, "What harm can the kid do?" The OK came through, and Jack Lucas, pageboy boss, gave me the good news. No announcing fee, of course, just the honor, as I wasn't a member of AFTRA (American Federation of Television and Radio Artists). Frank Butler, one of my favorite staff announcers, gave me some basic advice: "You'll be a little tense at first. But just relax and give the news. If you flub, keep going; don't go back over it. It only calls attention to it. Unless you give a wrong number, then it needs correcting. Just say: 'Here's that number again.' You'll do fine." It was sure nice to have someone like Frank Butler in your corner.

To evaluate my on-air performance, Dr. Ziebarth gave my speech class an assignment. My classmates were to stay up the following night – on a Saturday night – to hear me read the news, then critique me. (They sure liked that idea. And I thought they were my friends.) Nervous? No. Just scared. Who wouldn't be, knowing the 50,000 watt clear channel station's coverage was awesome, to say the least. It boomed out at night to some 38 states. WCCO had many regular listeners as far away as Omaha, Denver, and New Orleans. And I know it reaches western Wisconsin, as I received a fan letter from Ted Johnson, a dairy farmer from Siren, Wisconsin. I had met Ted at the WCCO exhibit at the Minnesota State Fair, just a few weeks before. "See," he wrote. "I told you at the fair that I would hear your voice sometime on WCCO." Ted went on to say that he was in the dairy barn milking cows when my early morning newscast came on. (Besides the midnight news, they had me read some early morning newscasts, also.)

Station Tours
Radio fans loved seeing the WCCO studios

We pageboys were well schooled in giving station tours. Jack Lucas had us practice our presentation until it was perfect. "Pretend your mother is in the group," Jack used to say. "Wouldn't she expect the best from you?" That Jack! He sure knew how to motivate us. Listeners would call and ask if they could see the station. It was good PR to know our fans better. We gave group tours of ten or more. One of the largest groups I had was a ladies circle of about 25 from Mount Olivet Lutheran Church in south Minneapolis. I greeted the ladies at the reception desk, and took them first to WCCO's trophy wall. (Which is pretty impressive.) I pointed out the Marconi and Peabody awards, and explained they weren't given out lightly. And that winning the award for "Best Station," was quite an accomplishment.

Next, we visited the various studios and I spelled out what they were used for. The most frequent asked question was: "Where does Cedric Adams give his newscast?" One white haired lady wondered which studio broadcast the *Ma Perkins* soap opera. That's when I explained the difference between local and network programs. I took them past one of the radio booths where there would always be a staff announcer on duty. From the hallway they were able to see and hear Howard Viken give a station break. You should have seen the smiles when Howard's familiar voice came through the speaker. They'd be telling their friends about that one, for sure.

Another tour highlight was the newsroom. It's the heart of the station, with lots of activity. There were always phones ringing, typewriters, and teletype machines clacking, and police monitors squawking. And newsmen were rushing to meet deadlines. Harry Reasoner, newswriter, allowed me to let the tour groups look over his shoulder to read the copy he was banging out. The Church ladies noticed that Harry didn't type the conventional way. They were right. Harry used the old H & P typing system – hunt and peck. He typed with his two index fingers, and was as fast and accurate as a legal secretary. I told the group to tune in for the Noontime News with Cedric Adams at 12:30 p.m., and they'd hear those same words they read earlier in the day, in Harry's typewriter.

The 30-minute tour concluded in the fourth floor auditorium, where the *Saturday Nite Radio Party* was held. This always took about ten minutes, because there was so much to see on the stage. I told them about Gene Autry broadcasting his *Melody Ranch* the week before. Some of the ladies had heard the program, and couldn't believe they got to step on the very same stage that the famous radio and movie star, Gene Autry, had broadcast from. At tour's end, I gave each of the ladies a WCCO 25th Anniversary booklet, which was a nice way to cap off the tour. A few days later, Jack Lucas showed me the note the Church group had written in appreciation of the tour. My name was mentioned, and it went up on the bulletin board for the world to see.

Fastest Gofers On Earth
"Coffee? Sandwich? Don't fret. We'll fetch!"

Not everyone is wired to be a gofer. (Go for this; go for that...) Some folks can't handle menial, or what may appear to be, meaningless tasks. But it was part of our pageboy job, so we prevailed. Station personnel had us going every which way. The producers kept us the busiest. They had us running prior to airtime. There were four of them: Bob Sutton, who was the program director, and married to Ramona Gerhard, Bill Shepherd, Jerry Nelson and Bob McKinsey. There were always nagging problems, or headaches, right before show time. Maybe the producers needed another script, or wanted studio equipment moved. Or, have us round up the missing talent. And when the Bayer bottle was running low, we knew where to find the aspirin. One time Jerry Nelson's stopwatch was failing. (A producer's stopwatch is akin to a carpenter's hammer.) Quick as a wink I borrowed one from another producer whose program wasn't quite as critical. Announcers were different. They wanted a constant flow of fresh brewed coffee, or a pack of cigarettes. If their blood sugar was low, they needed a quick ham and cheese on rye, from Freddie's, a popular restaurant and watering hole. (Just two doors north of the station, next to the Minneapolis Athletic Club.)

Now that I think about it, we weren't gofers. We pageboys were fixers and problem solvers. It's no wonder we "ran" the station. Well nearly. Actually, the station ran itself.

"Saturday Nite Radio Party"
WCCO's musical extravaganza rivaled Broadway

WCCO owned Saturday night. The station had the lion's share of listeners with its popular *Saturday Nite Radio Party*. As one media critic described the event: "It was a live musical extravaganza that rivaled Broadway. And it was free." If you were lucky, you had a ticket to see the live shows. From 7–9:00 p.m. fans from all over Minnesota packed the 700-seat, fourth floor auditorium. "Radio Party" was the umbrella for a two-hour bloc of 30-minute live programs in prime time, including Cedric Adams' *Stairway to Stardom*, sponsored by McGarvey Coffee. Another, for the country western fans, was *The Red River Valley Gang*, with Bob DeHaven, and sponsored by Robin Hood Flour. It was WCCO's version of Nashville's *Grand Ole Opry*, a lively, toe-tapping, fiddle-fast program. All in western costume, too. Sally Foster was the girl singer, and reminds me now of Dolly Parton. Sally was married to Earl Steele, a staff announcer.

Saturday night was the busiest night for pageboys. First, we had to get the auditorium ready for broadcast. This required dressing the stage with signage and positioning the risers and music stands, just so. Next, we guided the hundreds of guests to WCCO's fourth floor auditorium and seated them. Minutes before airtime we stood by for further instructions from the show producers. Maybe it was a microphone to adjust, sign to fix, or coffee to fetch. I swear! The station ran on coffee. WCCO is where I developed my five cup-a-day habit.

On the tiny stage, WCCO's big 20-piece orchestra featured some of the finest musicians in the trade. They could play whatever style of music you placed on their music stand. When not on the air, they had plenty of outside gigs that kept them busy. As Wally Olson, orchestra leader, told me, the Twin Cities rewarded its musicians with year-round work. Besides their shows at WCCO, there were concerts, recording sessions, nightclubs, ballrooms, parties, and functions of all kinds to keep a pay check coming in. The audience knew many of WCCO's musicians by name: Wally Olson, orchestra leader, Willie Peterson – who married Jeanne Arland – Ernie and Hal Gavin, Biddy Bastien, Dick Link, Ramona Gerhard, and others. Singers were Jeanne (Arland) Peterson, Sally Foster, Mary Davies, Tony Grise, and Burt Hanson. And, for the frosting on the cake, WCCO featured Hollywood and radio stars, like Rosemary Clooney, Mel Torme, Dennis Morgan, Gary Moore, The McGuire Sisters and The Chordettes. That's why the fans – mostly women – were willing to wait hours to attend the station's *Saturday Nite Radio Party*. Without a doubt, it was the finest two hours in entertainment you could find.

One February Saturday night the guest celebrity was Mel Torme. He sang two of his big hits. First, was *Again*, from the movie *Road House*, with Ida Lupino and Cornel Wilde. His encore was *Blue Moon*, from the MGM film he had recently appeared in, *Words and Music*. The WCCO audience gave him a warm welcome on that cold winter night. It seemed to motivate Mel to sing the best I've ever heard him.

Goof-Up of the Month
You tried <u>not</u> to win this award

I report with admirable modesty, that I won the pageboy's first "Goof-Up" Award. I won it because Larry Fisk, chief engineer, reprimanded me for crossing the line, and performing an illegal engineering function. I was in the engineer's tool and maintenance shop in the basement, rounding up microphones, cords, and equipment for the Tuesday night St. Paul remote, *Quiz of the Twin Cities*. Then, Mr. Fisk entered. "Do you have a union card?" he snapped, as I was loading the toolbox. "No sir," I meekly replied and explained that Harry Larson, the show's engineer, was running late, and called and asked me to do it for him.

"That's no excuse. And that's not the way we do things around here," added Fisk. "You get a hold of Mr. Larson and tell him to load his own equipment. He's the engineer, not you." Upon hearing about the incident, Jack Lucas, my boss, understood that I was young and eager, and was caught up in the middle of the situation. Like a good first sergeant, he stood up for me. But he did bring me up to speed on the consequences of infringing on union jurisdiction. Which has stuck with me to this day.

It made me feel better when my good buddy, Robert Vaughn, was the next recipient of the award. It seems Robert was on assignment to deliver the Saturday night news copy to Cedric Adams' home in Edina. He got lost. Terribly lost. He never made it in time for the remote broadcast. As a result, back at the station, the announcer on duty, Jack Huston, had to substitute for Cedric. That's the last time Robert had that assignment. They gave it to me. But had me make a practice run.

Jack Lucas must have invented the flexible hour system. He carefully scheduled my hours around my classes, first at Brown Radio School, then the University of Minnesota. I worked early mornings, 6-8:00 a.m., then after school, from 4-10:00 p.m. For study time, Jack gave me some switchboard duty when calls were few and far between. In his early 30's, he was a cool boss, and a good father figure for us. He was never demanding, or came unglued if we goofed-up.

Escorting the VIP's
Pageboys welcomed the celebrities to Minnesota

On a late Friday, I got the assignment to meet the Hollywood singing star, Dennis Morgan. He was flying in to the old Wold Chamberlain Field airport for a Minneapolis Aquatennial broadcast. I was anxious to meet him as his visit meant another big name in my autograph book. (My collection was growing since I joined WCCO.) I was told he was the highest paid singer on the Warner Bros. lot. Hurrying to our motor pool, I checked out the station's spiffy 1948 DeSoto station wagon. (I loved that vehicle. I wish Chrysler, back in 1960, had kept DeSoto and dropped Dodge.)

Dressed in my dress blues I met Mr. Morgan at his receiving gate. Tall, tanned and movie star good looking, he was easy to spot. I was nearly blown away when I saw how young he looked, as he had to be in his forties. (From a teenager's perspective, someone in their forties was ancient.) I gave him a warm Minnesota welcome, and he never stopped smiling. (As he did in all his films.) He did most of the talking asking about this and that. I told him I enjoyed his role in *Hollywood Canteen*, which included most of the Warner Bros. Studio, including Betty Davis and John Garfield. He picked up on my interest in Hollywood, and that *really* got him talking. "You must see lots of films," he said. "But I bet you can't name five of mine," he challenged.

"Bet I can," I answered. Oh, oh, I thought. Now I've done it. I don't think I've seen five of his movies. "Well, I already named one, I've only got four to go," I reminded him. He agreed. I was a movie nut, and hooked on double features, too. Now I had to put on my thinking cap. As we sped back to the station, I was running out of time. I couldn't name another four, but I did get two more, *God Is My Co-Pilot*, and one with Eddie Cantor and Dinah Shore, *Thank Your Lucky Stars*. He seemed pleased and considered me a good fan of his.

There's more to the story. While Dennis Morgan was performing in Minneapolis, Doris Day, who made a splash in her first movie, singing, *It's*

Magic, in Warner's *Romance on the High Seas*, was filming *Tea for Two*, with Gordon MacRae. This film helped make her Warner's hottest singer, knocking Dennis Morgan out of his catbird seat. Oh, well, that's the way show biz works.

That lucky Robert Vaughn. He got to escort some of Arthur Godfrey's songbirds back to the station. They were Lu Ann Simms and The McGuire Sisters. They were coming in for a nationwide Aquatennial show to be held at the old Minneapolis Auditorium. The McGuire Sisters – Christine, Dorothy, and Phyllis – were just getting started on the Godfrey program. Their big hits, on Coral Records, a subsidiary of Decca, *Sincerely* (1954), and *Sugartime* (1956), were a few years away. And no disrespect, but we're still waiting for a number one hit from Lu Ann Simms. Her biggest one, on Columbia Records, was *Red Roses and Little White Lies* (1955).

When prying Robert for info about his pretty passengers, he said that the singers were quiet at first, but opened up when he told them he had their records. He also revealed his dream of going to Hollywood, and got a few chuckles from them. I wonder what they thought when they first saw *The Man from U.N.C.L.E.*, with Robert Vaughn in the lead role?

There was a strong bond between Arthur Godfrey and WCCO. Godfrey was a big admirer of Cedric Adams, and featured him as a substitute on his *Talent Scouts* TV show. A natural salesman on radio, Godfrey moved "tons" of product for his sponsors. Lipton Tea, I remember, was just coming out with their flow-through tea bag, that was a pretty big deal for tea lovers. The four-sided bag produced more flavor, faster, than the traditional two-sided bag. As his morning show was simulcast on radio and television, the TV audience got to see the tea bag demonstration, while the radio audience had to "imagine" it. But it must have worked, because Lipton sold millions of their new flow-through tea bags.

Godfrey loaned out many of his stars for WCCO's special programs, including: Frank Parker, Janette Davis, Marion Marlowe, Lu Ann Simms, The Chordettes, and The McQuire Sisters. It was a coup for WCCO to feature national talent, and it was good exposure for Arthur Godfrey's people to appear as featured performers. Incidentally, Godfrey received negative publicity when he fired Julius La Rosa. La Rosa went on with mild success with his own TV show and hits on Cadence Records. (A new label that Archie Bleyer, former musical director on the Godfrey Show, started up.) As you probably knew, The Arthur Godfrey Show was a launching pad for many artists in the music business, including The McQuire Sisters and The Chordettes, who appeared on WCCO, during their salad days.

Honor Bound
Pageboys couldn't be bribed or bought

I may have been the only person to say "No," to Mr. Max Winter, successful business executive, and former president of the Minnesota Vikings. Here's the story that has never been told before. One Wednesday afternoon when I reported for work, there was a message waiting for me from Mr. Max Winter, owner of the 620 Club, famous for its turkey-only menu, on Hennepin Avenue, in Minneapolis. He may have been small in stature, but he was a big thinker when it came to business. A sports enthusiast, he was part of the financial group responsible for bringing an NFL expansion team to Minnesota in 1960. (The Dallas Cowboys also came in to the National Football Conference that year.) Mr. Winter served as president of the Minnesota Vikings from 1965-1987. But back to the story. He wanted me to meet him at the Minneapolis Club on Second Avenue, just a few blocks south of the station. While walking there, I wondered what it was all about. He was one of the four panelists on *Let's Get Together*, a popular question and answer game show on the station. It aired on Thursday evenings, 7:30-8:00 p.m. Stew MacPherson was the host, and Gluek's beer the sponsor.

When he spotted me in the lobby, he waved and invited me to have a seat. My first impression of him was that he smacks of success. He was wearing a gray, double breasted suit with a red power tie. He noticed me admiring his wingtips, that were the shiniest I'd ever seen. Then he asked: "Dick, you run off the scripts for *Let's Get Together*, don't you?"

"Yes, sir," I replied.

"I would like an advance copy for tomorrow night's show," he said. "And I'll give you five dollars for your help."

Surprised at his request, I told him I could not do it. He seemed a little surprised at my answer. (All the questions and answers were in the script.) Mr. Winter continued. "I have a little bet with a friend and I sure would like to answer all the questions correctly." It wasn't like he was trying to buy military secrets, but instinctively I knew he should not have the script. At least, not receive it from me. From his expression, I could tell that not many people ever said "No," to Max Winter. That's when I got up, turned on my heel, and did a perfect 180 straight back to the station. While trotting back, I weakened a little, and almost wished I wasn't so honor bound. I could have used the five dollars, as my checking account was bone-dry.

There's a happy ending to the story. Even without my help, Mr. Winter correctly answered all his questions the following night, and was one of the winners. I was happy for him. Today, in memory of him, The Minnesota Vikings have made him another winner by naming their headquarters building in Eden Prairie, after him: Winter Park.

Mailroom Duty
Pageboys learned that knowledge is power

Life belongs to the curious. The pageboy inquisitiveness, if tested, would rank right up there with teenagers in an Apple store. Our curiosity really got turned on when we worked the mailroom. We handled all the sealed, confidential memorandums, sponsor contracts, fan mail, paychecks, and routine letters that WCCO received via the U.S. Postal Service. (When a first class postal stamp cost three cents, and we had two home mail deliveries a day.) Now, we weren't gossips, so the information in those envelopes was safe with us. But we were only human. So, if there was something eye-catching, we might give it our extra attention. Like I did, reading a memo about a big change for Rolf Hertsgaard's 7:15 a.m. news, sponsored by Peter Paul Candy, makers of Mounds and Almond Joy candy bars. It followed the *CBS World News Roundup*, the nation's longest running radio network newscast, on the air since 1938. (It gave Rolf a nice lead-in audience.) Together, with both programs, WCCO had a powerful one-two punch in news coverage. And the news lineup continued at 7:30 a.m. with George Grim, news analyst and popular Minneapolis Star columnist.

When I was at the station, most of the newscasts were in 15-minute segments, as opposed to shorter versions, today, due to our "hurry-up" lifestyle. Some call it America's, "...give it to me quick," mode. Now, back to Rolf. He felt something was up, and asked me if I heard anything on the grapevine about his morning newscast. In the memo, I had learned that the sponsor wanted a bigger name delivering the news (i.e., Bob DeHaven). The program department did all they could to keep Rolf, as he was doing a good job. But Bob DeHaven got the nod, and would replace Rolf Hertsgaard in a week. I told none of this to Rolf, who was about to lose his program. Besides the prestige, Rolf would also lose his $15.00 per program talent fee. (DeHaven was to get $25.00.) Those talent fees may seem meager, today, but back then, in the 1950s, they would buy a nice dinner at Charlie's Café Exceptionale, just a few blocks east of the station, on Fourth Avenue. (One of the top eating spots in Minneapolis, along with Harry's and Murray's. Of the three, only Murray's is still in business.)

The sponsor was pleased with the switch, as DeHaven's popularity bumped the ratings for the 15-minute newscast. Being a professional, Rolf congratulated DeHaven, and went about his business. Rolf would leave WCCO five years later, in 1955, to become the most popular TV news anchor on WBAL-TV, Baltimore. The Hertsgaard name continued on 'CCO, though, when his son, Dan, worked at the station. Young Dan inherited his dad's voice qualities, and now is a free-lance artist. Rolf Hertsgaard died at age 81. The industry lost a great performer, and a real gentleman.

"Whoopee John Show"
Whoopee's mysterious fan letters still a mystery

Polka music was coming to WCCO. I was working the mailroom and learned about the new polka program in a memo. It was from the program department to Carl Ward, sales manager, requesting sponsors for the upcoming *Whoopee John Show*, Monday–Friday, 3:15-3:30 p.m. (To premier in September of 1950.) I wasn't exactly into polka music, myself, but I did know Whoopee John Wilfahrt (pronounced "Will-fert,") was a top performer. He was born in New Ulm, Minnesota's polka heartland. An artist on the accordion, he recorded for Decca and RCA Victor. He was known as "The Great One." Something unusual. He had two hits on one Decca 78 rpm record. It was a salute to the Twin Cities. Side "A" was *The Minneapolis Polka*. Flip side was *The St. Paul Waltz*. (A collector's record; this little gem is hard to find, as is his biggest hit, *Clarinet Polka*.)

Whoopee's fans were fantastic. They were as loyal as you'll find among any fan club. They bought his records. Wrote fan letters. And traipsed all over the region to attend his one-nighters, and polka the whole night through. Now they were going to hear him on WCCO Radio. But due to a last minute news special from the network, the premier show was preempted. Thus, no polka show on Monday. But what's this? Three postcards arrived on Tuesday, the following day, gushing how great Whoopee John's first program was. How could this be? There was no show on Monday. It was cancelled. Knowing something was fishy, I hand delivered the cards to Bob Sutton, program director. He studied them. Then, studied them some more. He smiled, and said it was a case of someone – probably Whoopee John – stacking the deck. He kept the postcards and said that things were pretty bad when talent had to write their own fan letters. Gosh, Whoopee didn't need to pull this stunt on the station. He didn't have anything to prove. He was already a success with nearly 1,000 recordings. Plus, he had a full booking on the polka circuit. His self-esteem must have been on the fritz.

The Whoopee John Show ran its scheduled 13-weeks, but was not renewed. During his stint on the station, I found myself warming up to the polka beat. As did the whole country when Perry Como crossed over from pop to polka in 1950, with his big hit, *Hoop-Dee-Do*, by Frank Loesser. (Even Doris Day recorded it.) Finally, Whoopee was getting some help from the pop field, playing his kind of music. The polka world lost "The Great One," Whoopee John Wilfahrt, in 1961. He died at the age of 68. To this day, we still don't know who sent those "mystery" fan letters to the station.

Robert Vaughn Goes Hollywood
From pageboy to "The Man from U.N.C.L.E."

No one at the station had any idea there was a future superstar on the pageboy staff. Robert Vaughn, my sidekick, vowed to make it big in the movies. A little like Joe Namath promising that his Jets team, a huge underdog, would beat the Baltimore Colts in the 1969 Super Bowl. Robert Vaughn delivered on his promise, too, and scored big in Hollywood. In his first movie, *The Young Philadelphians*, with Paul Newman, he won an Academy Award Nomination for Best Supporting Actor, playing a drug addict. Then he went on to the western classic, *The Magnificent Seven* with Yul Bryner, Steve McQueen, Charles Bronson and James Coburn. In 1964 he landed the plum TV role as Napoleon Solo in *The Man from U.N.C.L.E.*, the popular spy series, with David McCallum and Leo G. Carroll. Steve McQueen, in 1968, personally cast him as the police commissioner in the cop/car chase thriller, *Bullitt*.

Looking back, we pages should have known Robert Vaughn was Hollywood bound. For one thing, he came from a show business family. For another, he was a free spirit, and wouldn't be caught dead wearing his pageboy uniform. Lastly, take his sponsor that landed him his WCCO job. It was Ralph Bellamy, a friend of Robert's family, and a big name movie star.

From a letter I received, here are Robert Vaughn's early Minnesota memories, as published in the book, *Hooked On Minnesota*:

"My Minnesota memories are many. After graduating from North High School in 1950, I attended the University of Minnesota and worked at WCCO Radio as a pageboy. Working with the best in broadcast, I learned plenty. Harry Reasoner, a newsman writing Cedric Adams' newscasts, taught me the 'Rip and Read' theory; how to sight-read and be ready for live broadcasting. It helped me enormously in Hollywood during readings and auditions for movie and TV roles. I had the early-morning shift and kept Roger Krupp, a former NBC network announcer, loaded with hot coffee, before his announcing duties. Bob DeHaven used to kid me about dressing better than he did. (I always loved clothes.) I got in hot water once with Jack Lucas, boss of the pageboys. He assigned me to deliver the 10:00 p.m. news copy to Cedric Adams' home in Edina for a remote broadcast. Only problem was I had trouble driving the '48 Cadillac limousine – and got lost. After that, I believe the policy was to have backup copy at the station."

Robert Vaughn, movie and TV actor
Ridgefield, Connecticut

The pageboy class of 1951 is proud of Robert Vaughn and his achievements. Including his film, TV and stage work, academia life, and his autobiography, *A Fortunate Life*.

The Christmas Card
WCCO remembers a pageboy in Korea

It may not seem like a big deal to some people, but for me, the impact of that Christmas card from WCCO was enormous. It was in December of 1952 and the Korean War was still on. I was a Marine Radio Correspondent with the First Marine Division, and had just returned to my tent after interviewing some 7th Regiment Marines in reserve, putting on a Christmas show. The tape would be rushed to Hollywood, for airing on NBC's *The Marine Corps Show*, a musical/variety show, featuring radio and movie stars.

Mail is a priority with the Marines, and we received it several times a week. Mail call was pretty good to me that day. I got about five letters, and two boxes of cookies that were pretty beat-up, but at least eatable. And yes, it's true that you shared treats with your tent buddies. But that way you got some of the other guy's, too. I was in the P.I.O. tent (Public Information Office), with seven other combat correspondents; photographers, writers and radio correspondents. Most held rank on me – I was a corporal – as they were career Marines and had served in World War II.

It was easy to spot the Christmas card from WCCO, as the envelope had a bright red, white, and blue "VIA AIR MAIL" sticker that would assure faster delivery. And in the upper left hand corner was the return address: WCCO, Mpls. 2, Minn. (No zip codes then; just zone numbers for the cities.) I couldn't believe my eyes when I opened it. No ordinary Christmas card, this had signatures from all my pals back at the station. There had to be fifty names. Most used blue ink; some green, to make the card very colorful. It must have taken days to corral everyone to sign the card. I suspected it was Marlee (Michaelson) Ruane, record librarian, and Jack Lucas, pageboy supervisor, who organized the project. I would find out for sure when I got back home.

MSgt Joe Hensley, top dog, noticed my excitement, and asked what was so special. I showed him the card, and he recognized some of the names – Bob DeHaven, Larry Haeg, Burt Hanson, Gordon Eaton, Ed Viehman, Rolf Hertsgaard, and Howard Viken – as his wife, Betty, was from Minnesota, and he was acquainted with WCCO. "Be sure to save this card, Dick. With all those autographs it may be worth a million dollars in a few years," Joe smiled. I still have that momento. And Joe was right. It's worth a million dollars to me.

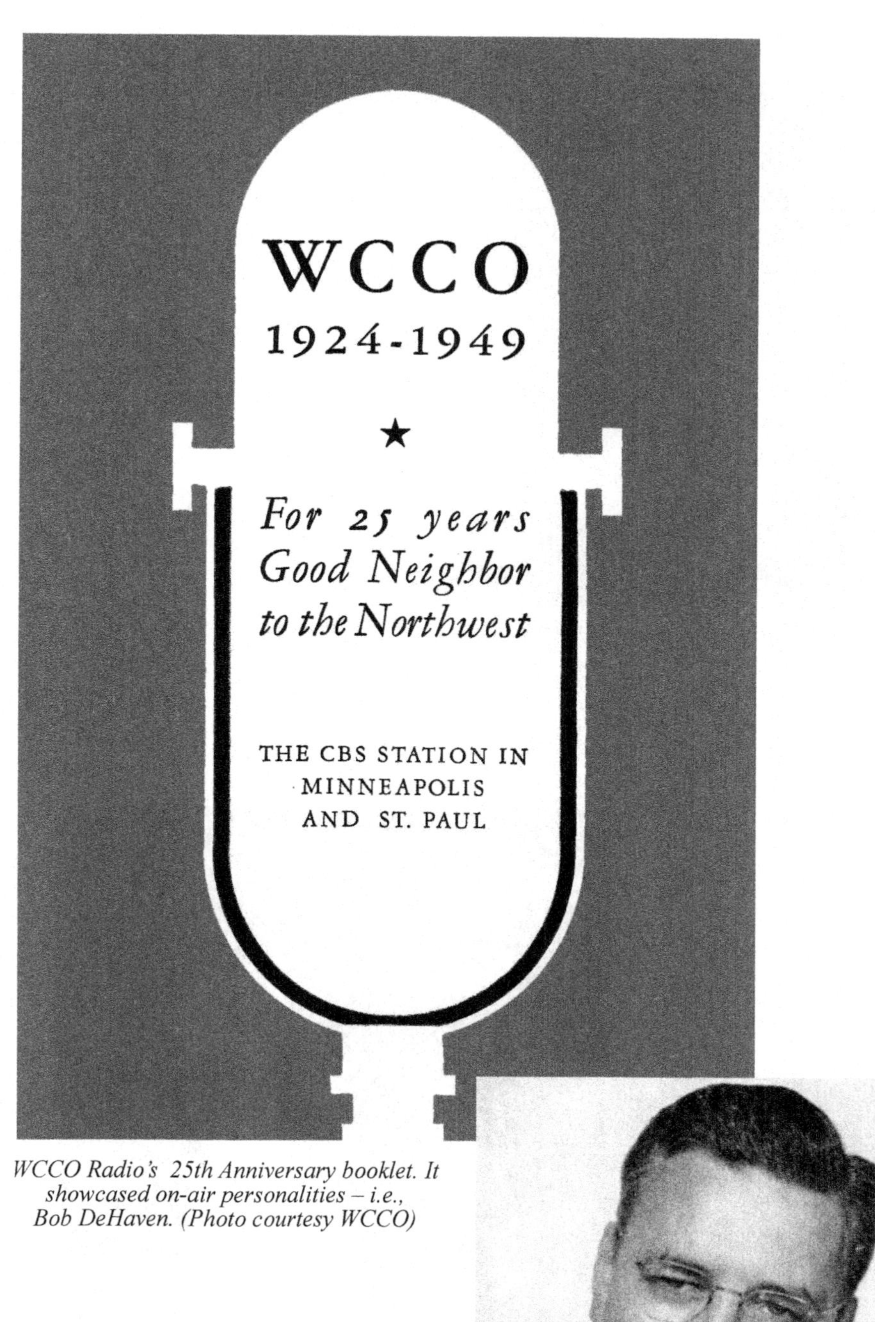

WCCO Radio's 25th Anniversary booklet. It showcased on-air personalities – i.e., Bob DeHaven. (Photo courtesy WCCO)

*Burt Hanson, Minneapolis' favorite tenor.
(Photo courtesy WCCO)*

*Sally Foster, featured singer on WCCO's "Red River
Valley Gang." (Photo courtesy WCCO)*

The author in a University of Minnesota Alumni Association promotional ad. (Photo courtesy University of Minnesota)

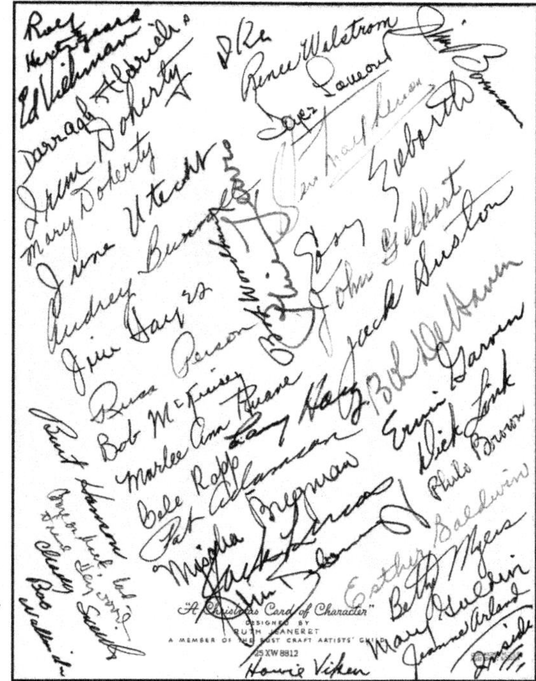

Collector's item! The author, serving in Korea in 1952, received Christmas card with WCCO's colleagues' signatures. Many names are now legends. (Author's collection)

Good news! The author, right, with Jack Lucas, pageboy supervisor, gets OK to read midnight news. (Photo courtesy WCCO)

Ted Williams, a Minneapolis Miller at Nicollet Park in 1938, gave the WCCO play-by-play announcers plenty to talk about. (Photo courtesy Minnesota Historical Society)

Harry Reasoner, WCCO newswriter. Later, on CBS' "60 Minutes."
(Author's collection)

Live music for the "Doughboy Country Journal." Seated at table: left, Gordon Eaton, announcer,
and Larry Haeg, host. Standing: Willie Peterson (at piano,) Mary Davies, Tony Grise,
Irv Wickner, Biddy Bastien, (accordionist unidentified,) Frankie Roberts, Ernie Garvin,
Burt Hanson, Hal Garvin and Dick Link. (Photo courtesy WCCO)

WCCO's On-Air

Bottom row: Paul Giel, Charlie Boone, Bob Allison, John Kundla, Dick Chapman, Franklin Hobbs. Second row: Ray Scott, Dr. E.W. Zebarth, Jim Hill, Jergen Nash, Maynard Speece, Clarence Tolg. Third row: Dick Enroth. Joyce Lamont, Bob DeHaven, Roger Erickson, Paul Jay, Halsey Hall, Herb Carneal. Top row: Arv Johnson, Sid Hartman, Howard Viken, Randy Merriman, Jim Bormann, and Gary Bennyhoff. (Photo courtesy WCCO)

Family in 1960s

Cedric Adams, left, with Eddie Cantor and Gary Moore, standing, at the 1950 "Minneapolis Aquatennial Show." (Photo courtesy WCCO)

Bernie Bierman, Golden Gopher head football coach, center, and sportscasters, Halsey Hall, left, and Sid Hartman, right. (Photo courtesy WCCO)

Clellan Card autographed his joke book for the author.
(Author's collection)

Jimmie Dodd, Mickey Mouse Club's
head Mouseketeer, with wife, Ruth,
and cat, Kiki. Autograph is to
Debbie Hill, the author's daughter.
(Author's collection)

Cedric Adams, Minnesota's first radio superstar.
(Photo courtesy WCCO)

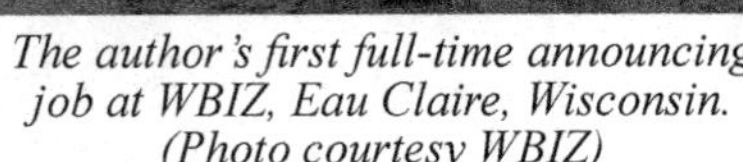

The Author tape records fairgoer at the 1950 Minnesota
State Fair, with helper, Pat Acre.
(Photo courtesy WCCO)

The author's first full-time announcing
job at WBIZ, Eau Claire, Wisconsin.
(Photo courtesy WBIZ)

The author "broadcasting" in Korea, as seen in "Leatherneck Magazine."
(Courtesy U.S. Marine Corps)

Ray Mithun, co-founder of
Campbell Mithun.
(Photo courtesy Campbell Mithun)

An early Land O' Lakes ad.
Campbell Mithun has had the
account for 80+ years.
(Photo courtesy Campbell Mithun)

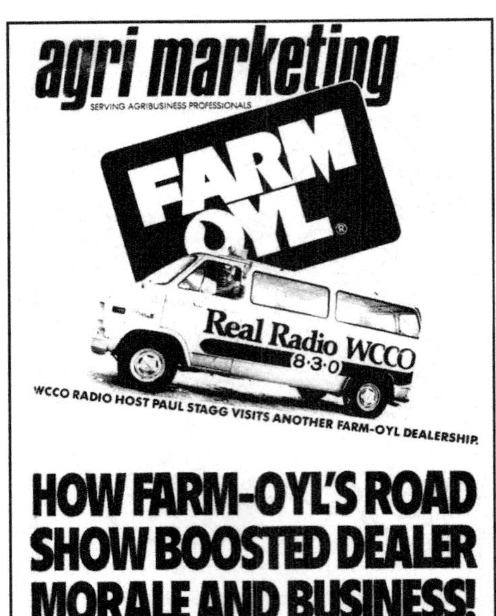

Agri Marketing magazine featured Farm-Oyl's Road Show, as heard on WCCO. (Photo courtesy WCCO)

Farm-Oyl's Road Show team. Left to right, Dick Hill, Farm-Oyl Company, WCCO personnel: Mary Ann Rentas, producer, Paul Stagg, announcer, Linda Paulson, publicity, and Brad Johnson, sales. (Photo courtesy WCCO)

-4-

WHEN DJ'S RULED THE AIRWAVES
Music! Music! Music!
Disc jockeys were the heroes of the day – and night

The 1950s were known as the "vinyl years." And WCCO played a major role in this colorful phase of radio. Originally called a gramophone, or vinyl record, the 78 rpm record (revolutions per minute), was shortened to "record." The LP (long play), or 33 1/3 rpm microgroove vinyl record, was developed in 1948, and was soon adopted in the 1950s as a new standard. (Hello LP's; goodbye 78's.) The records were being produced faster than the 2,500 nationwide disc jockeys could play them. The major record companies – Capitol, Columbia, Coral, Decca, Mercury, RCA Victor, and a new label, Cadence – rushed their latest releases to the stations. The records were complimentary. No charge. Free. Zip. The companies encouraged, begged, and sometimes, under the table, paid the DJ's to play them.

Because WCCO was a 50,000 watt clear channel station, and #1 in the marketplace, the record executives licked their chops and saw the station's potential – and dollar signs. They knew the WCCO DJ's influenced America's record sales. For a bonus, they made the recording artists available to the station. (Interviews with the artists helped spike sales.) WCCO had ten disc jockeys; all with a nice following. The ones I listened to most were Bob DeHaven (As Friendly Fred on *Friendly Time*), Ralph Moffatt (*Midnight* in *Minneapolis*), and Howard Viken and Joyce Lamont (*Dayton's Musical Chimes*). Viken also had his own record show in the late morning, which was quite popular. A few years after I left WCCO, Franklin Hobbs joined the station and made a big hit with his all night record program, *Hobbs House*. Prior, the station had signed off at 1:30 a.m.

"Goodnight, Irene"
A gut feeling made this tune #1

Sometimes it was nothing more than a gut feeling that excited a DJ about a new release. That's how it was with Howard Viken and *Goodnight, Irene*. He recognized its uniqueness, and played the dickens out of it. And helped make it a #1 smash hit. When I first heard it, I gave it a "thumbs down." You might know it. It zoomed to the top of the charts in 1950. The most popular version of *Goodnight, Irene*, was by Gordon Jenkins and The Weavers, a folk group on Capital Records. It's hard to believe, but 50 artists recorded it, including Frank Sinatra, whose version hovered near the top spot for awhile. The Weavers scored again with a follow-up tune, *On Top of Old Smokey*. If for some reason you've never experienced The Weaver folk songs, go to iTunes. As Howard Viken might describe their music: "It's got scratch." Here are the lyrics to *Goodnight, Irene*, as recorded by Gordon Jenkins and The Weavers:

> "Irene goodnight, Irene goodnight
> Goodnight Irene, goodnight Irene,
> I'll see you in my dreams.
> Last Saturday night I got married.
> Me and my love settled down.
> Now me and my wife have parted,
> I'm gonna take another stroll in town.
> Irene goodnight, Irene goodnight.
> Goodnight Irene, goodnight Irene,
> I'll see you in my dreams.
> Sometimes I live in the country,
> Sometimes I live in town.
> Sometimes I have a great notion
> To jump in the river and drown.
> Irene goodnight, Irene goodnight,

Goodnight Irene, goodnight Irene,
I'll see you in my dreams.
Ramblin' stop your gambling,'
Stop staying out late at night.
Go home to your wife and your family,
Sit down by the fireside bright.
Irene goodnight, Irene goodnight,
Goodnight Irene, goodnight Irene,
I'll see you in my dreams."

WCCO's Music Library
It took two people to manage all the records

Stacks of records were delivered to WCCO's doorstep everyday. To manage the station's thousands of records, there were two full-time librarians, Marilyn Myers and Marlee (Michaelson) Ruane. Besides unpacking and logging them in, they previewed and filed them. A big part of their job was making up the playlists for the station programs. They also auditioned the new releases for the DJs, and helped them pick music for their record programs.

Many of the new songs that came in were by unknown artists. (Until their records started taking off.) Such as Guy Mitchell, Johnnie Ray, Joni James, The Four Aces, Tony Bennett, and Eddie Fisher. After one play on their turntable, the librarians recognized the immense talent of Eddie Fisher. He entered the 1950s as a singing sensation. It seemed like every song he recorded became a hit. As they should, with Eddie's rich, booming voice, and dazzling arrangements and music tracks by Hugo Winterhalter. One Eddie Fisher tune that the WCCO DJ's frequently played, was *Wish You Were Here*. (It became #1 on the pop charts.)

While RCA Victor Records had big plans for their young, new singer, Liz Taylor had dibs on Eddie as her fourth husband. Eddie, at the time, was married to America's Sweetheart, Debbie Reynolds, but was singing his heart out to Liz. Now, please pay attention, as this gets complicated. Eddie dumped Debbie Reynolds in 1959, and married Ms Taylor. Then, Liz dumped Eddie for Richard Burton, and married him in 1964. The Eddie/Liz/Burton scandal – along with drugs and gambling – cost Eddie Fisher his career. Conversely, the scandal rekindled the careers of Liz Taylor and Richard Burton.

"Because of You"
Not every singer scores a #1 hit the first time

Anthony Benedetto was Italian, and had a nice baritone voice. Just made for pop music. To keep his voice in shape, he followed the old, Italian opera singing method – bel canto. He bounced around for a while, without any real success. Bob Hope advised him to change his name, and go see a major recording label. Columbia Records liked what they heard, and set up a recording session for the promising singer. Waiting for him in a Los Angeles recording studio, were a 25-piece orchestra, and some of the best brains in the business: Mitch Miller, producer, and Percy Faith, arranger and conductor. The song title on the young singer's music stand, read: *Because of You*. His fresh, natural style, with Percy Faith's lush orchestral arrangement, created a hit. *Because of You* reached #1 on the pop charts in 1951. Columbia Records was so pleased they went for an encore with, *Cold, Cold Heart*. (It was a pop crossover from the country song that Hank Williams wrote.) Two years later, in 1953, it was *Rags to Riches* and *Stranger in Paradise*. Four #1 records in three years. It was a fairy tale start for Tony Bennett's 50-year singing career.

Discovering Bob Newhart
Howard Viken helped launch a comedian's career

It's a tough way to start in the entertainment field. Maybe that's why not all stand-up comedians make it. Some that did: George Carlin, Robin Williams, Joan Rivers, Phyllis Diller, Rodney Dangerfield, Jerry Seinfeld, and Bob Newhart. Newhart got a push in his early days that launched his career. And it came from WCCO's Howard Viken. On his late-morning record show, Viken played and plugged Newhart's insanely funny monologue, *The Button-Down Mind of Bob Newhart*. (Newhart's niche was his deadpan humor.) The record sold well in Minnesota, and was the jump-start it needed to succeed nationally. It soon became #1 on the charts, and gave Newhart packed houses for his standup gigs. Then, Newhart did a classy thing. Living in Chicago, he made the 425-mile trip to Minneapolis to personally thank Howard Viken for his support. They became good friends. Newhart moved on to TV and films. His best TV show was playing a psychologist on *The Bob Newhart Show*, in 1972. It often ranked as the #1 TV show. Quite a leap from Newhart's early days, when, on some nights, there were fewer than 25 in the audience for his stand-up comedy routines.

I'm happy to report there was no payola among the WCCO disc jockeys, as occurred in New York. Seems some DJ's accepted money to push certain records in the Big Apple. The 1950s scandal shocked the broadcast industry, and was the subject of a Congressional Hearing. When the story broke, it blemished the music industry. But, like other shocking stories, payola was eventually forgotten, and the record industry continued to roll on. And the word, "payola," became part of our vocabulary.

The Top 40
WCCO's DJ's influenced America's record sales

Besides McDonald's, James Dean, and Rock and Roll, the Fabulous Fifties produced some memorable pop music. Here's the chart showing the songs most played in the 1950s, by WCCO disc jockeys. See how many of these top 40 tunes you identify with:

1. ***Wish You Were Here*** – Eddie Fisher
2. ***Mr. Sandman*** – The McGuire Sisters
3. ***Because of You*** – Tony Bennett
4. ***Love Is A Many Splendored Thing*** – The Four Aces
5. ***Goodnight, Irene*** – Gordon Jenkins & The Weavers
6. ***Bye Bye Love*** – The Everly Brothers
7. ***Young At Heart*** – Frank Sinatra
8. ***Music! Music! Music!*** – Teresa Brewer
9. ***Tennessee Waltz*** – Patti Page
10. ***Be My Love*** – Mario Lanza
11. ***Cry*** – Johnnie Ray
12. ***Wheel of Fortune*** – Kay Starr
13. ***Love Me Tender*** – Elvis Presley
14. ***Vaya Con Dios*** – Les Paul & Mary Ford
15. ***High Noon (Do Not Forsake Me)*** – Frankie Laine
16. ***Little Things Mean A Lot*** – Kitty Kallen
17. ***My Heart Cries For You*** – Guy Mitchell
18. ***Tenderly*** – Rosemary Clooney
19. ***Mona Lisa*** – Nat King Cole

20. ***Memories Are Made of This*** – Dean Martin
21. ***Bewitched, Bothered and Bewildered*** – Doris Day
22. ***Unchained Melody*** – Les Baxter
23. ***The Wayward Wind*** – Gogi Grant
24. ***Honeycomb*** – Jimmie Rodgers
25. ***April Love*** – Pat Boone
26. ***Harbor Lights*** – Sammy Kaye
27. ***On the Street Where You Live*** – Vic Damone
28. ***Crying In the Chapel*** – June Valli
29. ***Cherry Pink and Apple Blossom White*** – Perez Prado
30. ***You Belong to Me*** – Jo Stafford
31. ***It's All In the Game*** – Tommy Edwards
32. ***Mack the Knife*** – Bobby Darin
33. ***Why Don't You Believe Me*** – Joni James
34. ***Hoop De Doo*** – Perry Como & The Fontaine Sisters
35. ***You, You, You*** – The Ames Brothers
36. ***Lullaby of Birdland*** – George Shearing
37. ***Venus*** – Frankie Avalon
38. ***Theme from "A Summer Place"*** – Percy Faith
39. ***Moments to Remember*** – The Four Lads
40. ***Faraway Places*** –Margaret Whiting

All the pop singers took a big hit from Rock and Roll in the 1960's. For many, it was the end of their career. Others – like Frank Sinatra and Tony Bennett – wisely turned to the standards, theme albums, and live concerts. For Tony, it wasn't until the 1980's when he became "popular," again. Some of the girl singers – Margaret Whiting, Rosemary Clooney, and Helen O'Connell – made a smart marketing move. They formed a coalition, and took their show on the road. They each had their own segment on the stage, and performed their hits from the past. Audiences loved reliving the Golden Oldies Music.

How compelling are the pop standards? Bob Dylan, a folk rock artist, has a new album, "Shadows in the Night," featuring ten of Frank Sinatra's favorite songs. Even Dylan recognizes the power of pop music. This is one of the few times that Bob Dylan, singer-songwriter, raised in Hibbing, Minnesota, recorded a pop tune. The times. They sure are a-changin'.

"Friendly Time"
Not many knew who Friendly Fred really was

Bob DeHaven was one of the top disc jockeys in the industry. But not everyone knew it, because he was always identified as "Friendly Fred," on *Friendly Time*. DeHaven didn't try to disguise his voice, but spoke in a relaxed manner to match the program's theme. It was a new on-air style for DeHaven, and showed his versatility. His program ran 10:30-11:00 p.m., Monday-Friday, and was sponsored by Grain Belt, "the Friendly Beer." The 30-minute format forced him to make every minute count, while other disc jockeys had hours to spin their records.

Bob DeHaven, alias Friendly Fred, used a clever way to open his show. Instead of a theme song, he played a portion of his first tune as an opener. Then, he gave the formal program opening and completed playing his first selection. Fans liked this unique opening. During commercials, listeners heard beer being poured, and could almost "see" a nice cold glass of Grain Belt Beer. (Radio is excellent with sound effects, and in this instance, it helped the sponsor sell more six packs.)

DeHaven was picky about his playlist, and picked big doses of Perry Como, Margaret Whiting, George Shearing, Rosemary Clooney, and Percy Faith. Besides being a popular DJ at night, Bob DeHaven was a program host, newscaster, and one of WCCO's top headliners. He loved performing in front of an audience, such as *Quiz of the Twin Cities*. A media critic noted that of all the station on-air personalities, DeHaven best personified the "Good Neighbor" spirit of WCCO. He died in 1990 at age 81, and was inducted into the Minnesota Broadcasting Hall of Fame in 2010.

"Hobbs House"
Late nighters tuned in for their music fix

The big band sound was so successful on Franklin Hobbs program, that he stuck with it for 20 years. Franklin was host of *Hobbs House*, which aired weekdays from 11 p.m.–5:00 a.m. Many of his fans listened to him for the full 20 years, while he was on the air (from 1959-1979). Not many DJ's have that kind of staying power, to last two decades in the same time slot, and on the same station. But Franklin did, because he "wore" like a favorite pair of leather slippers. His voice was as smooth and rich as his music. Some women tuned in just to hear Franklin Hobbs speak, and give commercials. Music lovers tuned in to learn what was cool on the music scene. Over the road truckers discovered that *Hobbs House* helped them stay awake during a cross-country run. Teenagers and young adults were fans, also. They turned on the dreamy music for their dance and slumber parties. And for dates in their daddies' Dodge.

Right from the get-go, you knew Franklin favored the big band sound. It wasn't many minutes into the show, when you heard some Glenn Miller, Tommy Dorsey, or Harry James. Or, maybe it was Benny Goodman, Artie Shaw, Ray Anthony, or Charlie Barnet. It's what the bulk of the audience tuned in for. Much of the music came from his private collection, which was extensive. A perfectionist, Hobbs also showcased the best in singers, including: Frank Sinatra, Nat King Cole, Tony Bennett, Mel Torme, Billy Eckstine, and Ray Charles. Franklin featured plenty of talented girl singers, too. Such as Peggy Lee, Jo Stafford, Helen Forrest, Helen O'Connell, Billie Holiday, Sarah Vaughan, and Ella Fitzgerald. The music coming from *Hobbs House* was like a Who's Who of top musicians in the recording industry.

With a six-hour format to work with, Franklin Hobbs had the luxury of drawing from all shades of the music spectrum. He needed about 70 records for his show. Franklin didn't play just vanilla. Some tunes jumped. Jumped – like Les Brown's *Leap Frog* – to keep listeners awake. After all, it was the wee small hours of the morning when his show ran. Many listeners benefited from Franklin's subtle music appreciation offerings. For example, not all of us like country music. To show that country has its place, every so often Franklin would slip in a Willie Nelson, Johnny Cash, or Marty Robbins. Or, Loretta Lynn, Tammy Wynette, or Patsy Cline. Hobbs' salute to Nashville met with good response. Before you knew it, there were honest to goodness conversions to country. (Country can grow on you if you don't watch out.)

For the true jazz lover, Franklin Hobbs would unlock his jazz collection and bring out the classic Capital album No. 167, Stan Kenton's *Artistry In Rhythm*. But before spinning it, Franklin would explain Kenton's intention, as many listeners were in the dark – or worse, turned off – by Stan Kenton's innovative jazz sound. So, using salesmanship, Franklin Hobbs explained the features and benefits, and converted many of his listeners to different styles of music. Beyond pop, he wanted his fans to experience all the genres of music (i.e., blues, country, Dixieland, folk, jazz, Latin, R&B, and rock). And like the expert he was, he pointed out the little nuances – such as phrasing and breathing – that made Frank Sinatra, Ella Fitzgerald, and Tommy Dorsey, so great. You got your money's worth when you went to *Hobbs House.*

Oh, did I mention that Franklin Hobbs was a former actor and singer? His professional career in the entertainment field, gave him a leg up on other DJ's. He personally knew many of the big name celebrities that appeared on his show. His audience enjoyed hearing the latest Hollywood gossip, and getting inside information on the record industry.

Hobbs had loyal listeners all around the country. His show reached 38 states and parts of Canada, by virtue of WCCO's powerful 50,000 watt clear channel station. His following was diverse, to say the least, as this audience profile shows: stay at home fans, musicians, over the road truckers, folks in cars, and all night workers (i.e., manufacturing, gas stations, hotels/motels, dance halls, cafes, diners, and taverns). One media critic, who praised Franklin Hobbs for his lifetime achievements, estimated that some 360,000 records were played on *Hobbs House*, during its 20 year run. That's entertainment, man! Franklin Hobbs passed away in 1995, at the age of 75. He was inducted into the Minnesota Broadcasting Hall of Fame in 2007.

Minnesota's Mona Records
Ramona & Burt released their first record – "Because"

A new venture is always exciting to hear about. Especially when you're part of it. In 1950 there was a new record label in Minnesota, Mona Records. Ramona Gerhard and Burt Hanson created the new record company, named after Ramona. On their first 78 rpm single, side A was *Because*, and the flipside was *My God And I*. Both were favorite songs with the public, and sold quite well. I know, because I helped distribute the recordings all over the state. In addition to my pageboy duties, Ramona, organist, and Burt, tenor, hired me to deliver their records to local and regional stores. (Dayton's, now Macy's, was the biggest buyer.)

Ramona and Burt had their own 30-minute show, and appeared on many other station programs. Besides radio work, they were well booked with personal appearances in the region. Ramona loved giving concerts. A native of Watertown, South Dakota, she studied music in Europe, and at MacPhail School of Music in Minneapolis. She was a whiz with the mighty Wurlitzer. (The same pipe organ used in movie theaters in the 1930's and '40's.) Burt Hanson, the area's most popular tenor, was a good match for Ramona's style, which made her so much in demand. She performed an annual Christmas concert in the Minneapolis Northwestern National Bank's atrium. Downtown workers took an extra long lunch hour to enjoy the holiday event.

After their recording session, it was my job to take the master tape to a local disc manufacturer to produce 1,000 copies on 78 rpm vinyl records. As sales were brisk, more pressings were made and kept me busy. With advance orders from music and department stores, I started my deliveries. I went as far north as Duluth; as far south as Rochester. Working for Mona Records was a great business experience for me. And a nice surprise was the $50.00 Christmas bonus I received in 1950, from two of my favorite artists, Ramona and Burt. Thanks to them, my bone-dry checking account was finally in the black.

"Midnight In Minneapolis"
A smoky end to Ralph Moffatt's record program

Many nights after reading the midnight news, I stuck around to shoot the breeze with Ralph Moffatt, late night disc jockey. After one of his shows ended at 1:30 a.m., I was getting ready to go home. Then it happened. The studio lights went out and we both smelled smoke. "Oh, my God! The station's on fire," I hollered. Here's the rest of the story from the *Minneapolis Star* on January 25, 1951:

WCCO BUILDING FIRE
"Midnight in Minneapolis"
Has Dark, Smoky Sequel

"MIDNIGHT IN MINNEAPOLIS," a musical reverie, was followed by a "lights out" drama in the WCCO studios at 1:30 a.m. today.

The lights went out while Ralph Moffatt, disc jockey, who had signed off the station with "Midnight," was having a chat with Dick Hill, a pageboy.

In the blackness of the studio, which has no windows, the two lit matches and inched their way into the second-floor corridor of the five-story WCCO building at 625 Second Avenue S.

The smell of smoke in the corridor gave them their first clue to the cause of the black-out, and they made haste to reach the street via a stairway.

On the way down they met firemen coming up. A passerby had seen smoke billowing out of a window and had called the fire fighters.

The firemen, after a fast survey, found smoke on all the five floors, but no fire. They sent in a second alarm at 1:40 a.m.

But even with reinforcements the fighters couldn't find the blaze in the dense smoke. They put in a third alarm and the search bore fruit.

The blaze broke out in a paint room in the basement and burned electric cables. Radio transmitter wires were not affected.

The flames had fizzled out but smoke lingered on and rose through the elevator shaft to fog the five upper floors. Firemen finished their work at 5 a.m.

Fire damage was slight, but several commercial shops in the building suffered smoke damage, the fire department said.

After the WCCO fire story ran in the *Star*, Ralph Moffatt and I were treated like heroes. The staff patted us on our backs, literally, and were curious about our ordeal. They had lots of questions: "What were your thoughts when the lights went out?" "Any smoke damage to your lungs?" "Did you really crawl down those stairs?" "Heavens! You both could have died!" Our colleagues got a taste of the smoke, as it lingered in the station for several days before the cleaning crew could blow it out. The smoky night was soon forgotten, and eventually things got back to normal. ∎

-5-

FOUR SEASONS OF FUN

Festivals & Events

WCCO promotes Minnesota's community events

Nothing brings people together better than a hometown festival, or special event. And the best part, they're going on all the time in 'CCOland. Minnesota puts on more than 800 public happenings each year. From art fairs, outdoor concerts, county fairs, to the Duluth Polar Bear Plunge in Lake Superior. Some festivals feature beauty pageants and hometown parades with all the extras, including the local high school band. Many spotlight their veterans whom everyone likes to see and honor. Others have a rich tradition, such as the Minnesota State Fair (1859), St. Paul Winter Carnival (1886), and the Minneapolis Aquatennial (1940). WCCO would never say so, but its promotional efforts have helped establish many of these events.

To promote a local event as a public service, WCCO relies on a press release. The person in charge of publicity – for New Ulm's "Octoberfest," for example – sends out a press release to the media, including WCCO. If applicable, the news department includes it in a newscast. When possible, an event person is interviewed by Dave Lee or other on-air personality. For major events, WCCO conducts remotes (i.e., The Governor's Fishing Opener and the Minnesota State Fair). During the Cedric Adams era, the station produced 30-minute live programs celebrating the Minneapolis Aquatennial and St. Paul

Winter Carnival. Some of the live shows emanated from the old Minneapolis Auditorium, and were broadcast coast-to-coast on the CBS network. For the Governor's Fishing Opener, WCCO had numerous live reports from lakes all over Minnesota. Nearly every on-air personality was involved in one of the region's favorite events – the Minnesota Fishing Opener.

Here is a partial listing of the most notable on-going events, from all over the State:

- **St. Paul Winter Carnival** – January
- **Art in Bloom,** Minneapolis Institute of Arts – May
- **Minnesota Fishing Opener** – Early May
- **Grandma's Marathon**, Duluth – June
- **Edina Art Fair** – June
- **Minneapolis Aquatennial** – July
- **Taste of Minnesota,** St.Paul – July
- **Farmfest,** Redwood County – August
- **Uptown Art Fair,** Minneapolis – August
- **WE Fest,** Detroit Lakes – August
- **Itasca County Fair,** Grand Rapids – August
- **Minnesota State Fair** – Late August to early September
- **Minnesota Renaissance Festival,** Shakopee – August to early September
- **Anoka's Grand Day Halloween Parade** – October
- **Octoberfest,** New Ulm – October
- **Minnesota Deer Season Opener**- Early November

Minnesota State Fair
One of the world's largest, finest expositions

The Minnesota State Fair is all Minnesota showcasing agriculture, art, and industry. The Great Minnesota Get-Together offers Twelve Days of Fun, ending Labor Day. Started in 1859, it is one of the world's largest, most visited expositions, with an annual attendance of over a million people. And each year there's a challenge for the food vendors to develop new "food on a stick " ideas. (Have you tried shrimp on a stick, yet? Or, a pickle dog?) The food craze started 70 years ago with the "Pronto Pup," which is still a favorite among fairgoers.

The State Fair is successful because it truly reflects the popular culture and concerns of the day. WCCO Radio has been a close "partner" for all of its 90 years in broadcasting. Besides actively promoting it, the station is an active exhibitor and draws thousand of fairgoers to its popular booth each year. The fair made international news when Teddy Roosevelt, on September 2, 1901, made his famous "Carry a big stick," speech. Politicians continue to come, as they have the opportunity to greet potential voters, face-to-face.

In 1949, WCCO made history at their exhibit in the Horticulture Building. Visitors to the Minnesota State Fair saw and heard, broadcasting's latest invention: reel-to-reel audio tape recorders and magnetic tape. The station put on a demonstration that allowed fairgoers to have their voices recorded and hear them played back. They were amazed at the new technology. As an announcer in training, I did most of the demonstrations. Fairgoers are inquisitive people. They spent extra time at our exhibit, learning all they could about the new tape recorders and asking how the new technology affected them. From all the smiles, I could tell it was one happening they'd share with friends.

During the demonstration, we showed how reel-to-reel tape recorders were changing the way radio stations operated. Prior, most programming was "live." A few programs were still recorded on 33 rpm records, or electrical transcriptions (ET's, as they were called). Magnetic audio tape was developed in Germany, and offered better quality than records. Plus it could be easily edited. Bing Crosby started the trend with his *Kraft Music Hall* program. Soon, taped programs were commonplace. It allowed WCCO to pre-record shows at its convenience, and broadcast them later. The best part, the taped program sounded "live." Listeners couldn't tell the difference. And Minnesota played a major part in the new technology, as St. Paul's 3M Company was a leader in this field, producing 3M's Scotch Brand Magnetic Tape. (The very tape I used in Korea several years later as a Marine Radio Correspondent.)

Tape technology soon expanded to the consumer market. And because motorists love their music, nearly every automobile and pick-up truck sported a tape player. First were the bulky 8-Tracks, then came the cassettes. Today's digital technology has replaced tape with CD's. What's next?

The Minneapolis Aquatennial
Celebrating the Ten Best Days of Summer

Something Minneapolis has going for itself, is the Minneapolis Aquatennial. Founded in 1940, it's a weeklong event held in July celebrating "The Ten Best Days of Summer." It features Minneapolis' beautiful lakes, and has as many as 70 events for the public. To tell all America about this unique event, WCCO broadcast a special coast-to-coast Aquatennial Show in 1950, from the old Minneapolis Auditorium. Victor Borge, the piano maestro, and Georgie Jessel, stand-up comedian, were the main attractions in the 15,000 seat venue. Also starring were the recording stars from The Arthur Godfrey Show, Lu Ann Simms and The McQuire Sisters. Plus, there were WCCO Radio air personalities, and local acts. Tickets ranged from $1.20 to $6.00.

The first thirty minutes of the two-hour event was the CBS nationwide hook-up. It was broadcast on Saturday, July 18, 1950. It aired in prime time (8:00-8:30 p.m., Minneapolis time). Cedric Adams and Bob DeHaven were co-hosts, with Frank Butler as announcer. Bob Sutton, program director, produced the show. My job, as usual, was to standby in the control booth in case Bob Sutton needed something. On Sutton's cue, Bob Wallinder, engineer, switched on Frank Butler's mike. Butler, standing at center stage in front of a WCCO microphone, opened the program with his familiar, rich, network sounding voice:

> *"From Minneapolis, Minnesota, the City of Lakes, it's the WCCO Aquatennial Radio Show, with guest stars Victor Borge and George Jessel. With co-hosts Cedric Adams and Bob DeHaven. Also starring the lovely songbird from the Arthur Godfrey Show, Lu Ann Simms. Plus, Arthur Godfrey's great new vocal trio, The McQuire Sisters. And also appearing is Minneapolis' favorite tenor, Burt Hanson. To start the show, here's your congenial co-host, CEDRIC ADAMS..."*

After Frank's introduction, the Minnesota crowd applauded, whooped, and whistled. The show was on the air! And true to WCCO's style, it went without a hitch. If the WCCO performers were nervous on the national hookup, they sure didn't show it. The Aquatennial show promoted both Minneapolis' City of Lakes and Minnesota's Land of 10,000 Lakes to millions of CBS listeners. Many of them, that night, made a promise to visit Minnesota, the

Land of Sky Blue Waters. Needless to say, the Minnesota department of tourism couldn't have been happier with the show's outcome. They estimated that the Aquatennial broadcast was worth a million dollars in free publicity for the state.

In 1951, Bob Hope came to town to participate in another gala Aquatennial broadcast. The radio and movie entertainer make a big hit with his Minnesota fans. If you're a Hope fan, there's a new book on him, *Hope: Entertainer of the Century*. It's a biography by Richard Zoglin, published in 2014. (And selling like hotcakes.) ∎

-6-

PLAY-BY-PLAY CHAMPION

The Sports Station – 8-3-0

WCCO covered all the teams and bases

Long before all-sports stations, WCCO was the hottest ticket for play-by-play broadcasts. It started in 1933 with the Minneapolis Millers, a Triple-A team in the American Association, and a farm club of the Boston Red Sox. The announcers were Halsey (Holy Cow) Hall and Eddie Gallaher. For college games, WCCO added the University of Minnesota's Golden Gopher basketball, football, and hockey teams. Over the years, other WCCO sportscasters were: Herb Carneal, Merle Harman, Dick Enroth, Al Shaver, Ray Scott, Babe LeVoir, Brad Nessler, Marv Conn, Sid Hartman, John Gordon, and Ray Christensen. Christensen was known as the voice of the Golden Gophers. Over a period of 50 years, he broadcast 510 Gopher football games.

One sportscaster, Sid Hartman, has been with the station for 60+ years, and is still performing with sportscasts in the morning, and on *Sports Huddle* with Dave Mona, on Sundays. Hartman, who founded the Minneapolis Lakers basketball team, now the Los Angeles Lakers, celebrated his 95th birthday in 2015.

In 1961, WCCO took a giant leap to the big leagues. The station won the contracts for both the Minnesota Twins and Vikings. They broadcast the Twins games for 46 years. It's no wonder that WCCO and sports were synonymous with the Golden Age of Local Radio. Today, WCCO continues its play-by-play tradition on a smaller scale. It broadcasts the Timberwolves, (NBA), with Kevin Horton on play-by-play. Also, the University of St. Thomas football games in the Minnesota Intercollegiate Athletic Conference. Dave Lee performs the play-by-play, with Eric Nelson on color. WCCO's Sunday show, *Sports Huddle*, 9:30 a.m. – noon, with Sid Hartman and Dave Mona, has been on the air for 30+ years, and is one of the most popular sports shows in the region.

The Minneapolis Millers
The Millers were "major league" to fans

The Fourth of July was a red-letter day for the Minneapolis Millers. Starting in 1933, it meant a double header with its archrival, The St. Paul Saints. Both teams were in the American Association, Western Division, a Triple-A league. (One level below the major leagues.) The first game was played in the morning in Minneapolis; the second one moved to St. Paul later that afternoon. It was like New York's subway series. My dad, Lloyd Hill, whom seldom missed a Halsey Hall broadcast, called ours, "the streetcar series." Those not attending the games had WCCO Radio. Halsey Hall and Eddie Gallaher, made you believe you were there. *Wheaties*, Breakfast of Champions, was a long time sponsor of the Millers, just as Hamm's Beer was with the Twins.

Halsey was the first to notice him. He was a tall, lanky 20-year old kid from San Diego, California. He stood 6' 4," wore number nine, played right field, swung left, threw right, and batted fourth in the lineup. The Boston Red Sox had just recently signed Ted Williams, and sent him to their farm club in Minneapolis. They wanted to develop his batting, running, and fielding skills for the big leagues. As a Knothole Gang member, I saw Ted Williams play on Saturdays. I was eight years old and really into baseball. I had no idea our paths would cross again. But they did, 15 years later, in Korea. But that's another story. (See chapter 9, "Marine Radio Correspondent.")

Ted Williams gave Halsey Hall plenty to talk about. As a result, Williams became a huge draw, and helped fill Nicollet Park in 1938. (And helped

WCCO's audience grow, at the same time.) He performed like a champion, batting .336, and hitting 43 homers and to win the American Association's Triple Crown. Williams started the 1939 baseball season in Boston's Fenway Park, and went on to a successful 19-year career as one of baseball's greatest hitters. As expected, Ted Williams was elected to Baseball's Hall of Fame in 1966. His lifetime batting average was .344, with a career total of 521 homers. He was the last major league player to hit .400 in a season. And he was ours – for one whole season – as a Minneapolis Miller.

Other future major league stars that played with the Millers were, Willie Mays (1951), who went on to the New York Giants, and Carl Yastrzomski (1960), who became another Boston Red Sox legend. The Millers also produced a couple of good managers for the Twins. Bill Rigney, a Miller in 1954-1955, was Twins manager in 1970-1972. Gene Mauch played for the Millers in 1958-1959, and managed the Twins from 1976-1980.

The Minnesota Twins
WCCO Radio carried the games for 46 years

Upon the arrival of the Twins, the Millers folded after their 1960 season. Ironically, Ted Williams, the world-class slugger, had retired that very year. But the Twins' fans would get to see his team, the Boston Red Sox, play at old Met Stadium, in Bloomington. (Now at Target Field, Minneapolis, one of the nation's finest baseball venues.) Listeners grew close to Herb Carneal and Halsey Hall during the Twins broadcasts. Inevitably, when excited, Halsey would let out a "Holy Cow," during the game. It became his trademark and nickname. Herb Carneal was voted into Baseball's Hall of Fame in 1996. And he made it into the Minnesota Hall of Fame in 2004. Carneal was voted Sportscaster of the Year 20 times, by the National Sportscasters and Sportswriters Association.

They still talk about it. The 1991 World Series, with the Twins beating the Atlanta Braves in the seventh game, 1-0. Jack Morris was the winning pitcher, going the full ten innings. It's considered the greatest World Series, ever. The 1987 World Series was also fruitful for the Twins. Another full seven games, and the first series to be played indoors. (In the Hubert Humphrey Metrodome.) Underdogs to the St. Louis Cardinals, the Twins won the final game, 4-2.

Seven is the lucky number of Twins in Baseball's Hall of Fame: Rod Carew, Steve Carlton, Harmon Killebrew, Paul Molitor, Kirby Puckett, Dave Winfield, and Bert Blyleven. Paul Molitor is the current manager of the Twins.

When WCCO dropped the Minnesota Twins' broadcasts after a run of 46 years, some fans had a hard time adjusting to their successor, KSTP AM 1500. One of the reasons given, was because the games didn't sound the same, even with John Gordon, play-by-play announcer, moving to the new station. No disrespect to KSTP, but WCCO's loyal fans can be awfully loyal. My sister, Eileen (Hill) Blake, an avid Twins fan, had a hard time finding KSTP on her radio. Used to WCCO's 8-3-0, she had never gone that high before – 1500 kilocycles on the dial.

"The Bernie Bierman Show"
Gopher fans relived Saturday's game on Sunday

It had all the bells and whistles of a Super Bowl halftime show. And more listeners than you could shake a stick at. It was the *Bernie Bierman Football Show*, aired on WCCO, Sunday afternoons in the late 1940s and early 1950s. Sponsored by Juster's Clothing, the show featured Coach Bernie Bierman, Halsey Hall, Babe LeVoir, Ed Viehman, coaches, players, and phone guests from all over the country. (LeVoir played for Bierman in the 1930s, and was an All-American quarterback.) And to stir everyone up with the "Minnesota Rouser," and other spirited music, there was Wally Olson's live orchestra.

All cleaned and healed-up, the guest players looked spiffy in their white shirts and ties, as they gave their spin on the game. Just a few of the Golden Gophers who appeared were Leo Nomellini, guard, Clayton Tonnemaker, center, and Bud Grant, end. Bierman was proud of his great teams, and was the winningest coach we ever had. He took that old axiom to heart: "Just win, baby!" He achieved five national and seven Big Ten Championships. He also had five undefeated seasons.

With Bierman at the helm, the University of Minnesota had the leading football program in the nation. His star running back, Bruce Smith, won the Heisman Trophy in 1941. (The only Gopher to do it.) Tom Harmon, from Michigan, won it the year before, in 1940, with Minnesota's Sunny Franck as runner-up. Bruce Smith won a Columbia Pictures movie contract in 1942 for his football story, *Smith of Minnesota*. It premiered in Faribault, Minnesota, Smith's hometown. A sequel of sorts, it followed *Harmon of Michigan*, produced by Columbia in 1941. Both films were fairly successful. A side benefit, it nationally showcased Minnesota's winning football program, and the power of the Big Ten Conference.

Bernie Bierman was the recipient of numerous Coach of the Year awards, and was inducted into the College Football Hall of Fame in 1955. He finished his Minnesota 14-year coaching career at the end of the 1950 season with a .727 winning record. To put a perspective on his performance, Murray Warmath, who followed a few years after Bierman, had a winning average of .558 for his 18-year coaching career at Minnesota. We lost a great coach and sports legend when Bernie Bierman died in 1977, at age 82.

The Minnesota Vikings
Ray Scott put listeners on the 50-yard line

With the NFL expansion to Minnesota in 1961, WCCO won the first Vikings radio broadcast contract. And the listeners were big winners, too, with Ray Scott's play-by-play. He called the many exciting games the Vikes played in. Including the intense border rivalry games with the Green Bay Packers. And it was Fran Tarkenton, who - to avoid getting sacked – scrambled, and started a whole new fad in football. And it was coach Bud Grant who led the team to four Super Bowls, but sadly, no rings. The Vikings have a baker's dozen in the NFL Hall of Fame, whose numbers were repeatedly called: Cris Carter, Chris Doleman, Carl Eller, Jim Finks (General manager), Bud Grant (Head coach), Paul Krause, Randall McDaniel, Alan Page, John Randle, Fran Tarkenton, Mick Tinglehoff, Ron Yary, and Gary Zimmerman. Although not carrying the games today, Viking fans still get good coverage on WCCO, with team updates, news, and interviews.　　　　　　　　　■

-7-

<u>WCCO REINVENTS ITSELF</u>

Radio Was Changing

General format stations didn't fit the times

In its heyday, nearly every local radio was tuned to WCCO. It so dominated the market that the station followed you wherever you went: the super market, beauty parlor, drug store, bait shop – even the dentist's office. By every measurement – ratings, share of market, awards, sales, and profits – WCCO led the way in Minnesota broadcasting. But like Camelot, the Golden Days of Local Radio didn't last forever. In the 1960s, radio was changing, because listeners were changing. The need for full service format stations providing their communities a balance of music, talk, information, sports, and live entertainment, was not needed in the scheme of things. There were more day care centers, fast food restaurants, microwaves, and convenient foods, like "soup for one." More single parent households, also. The service economy expanded at the expense of manufacturing, shrinking the middle class. The economic ground began to shift under society's most stable unit – the family. The huge influx of FM stations, and the rise of rock, country and R&B, segmented music tastes, and split the market into unlimited choices for the listener. The listener became a more sophisticated consumer. And more information oriented.

With today's fragmented media world, WCCO has only a fraction of its heydays' audience; from an awesome 70% to 7% share of market, or listening audience. This huge slippage is not due to any incompetence on WCCO's part, but merely a sign of the times. Because of social and technological changes, WCCO took a giant free fall in the marketplace. The days of live 20-piece orchestras were over. So were the jobs for the smooth, golden voices of the staff announcers. Even the pageboys had to go. One critic referred to the station's dominance, or glory days, as a "media fluke." I dispute that, and call those glory days, "a media miracle." But a format change was imperative. So, WCCO, being a proven pioneer and trailblazer, found a new path – a new niche. They got themselves up, dusted themselves off, and reinvented themselves as a successful news/talk station. Today, WCCO is a perfect fit for the information age. And because we now live in a totally different media environment, their current 7% market share could be considered "awesome" in today's world. Importantly, WCCO Radio remains one of the most successful broadcast operations in the nation.

Talk Radio
WCCO welcomes your opinions and problems

No one knows exactly how Talk Radio started, but one media critic swears it happened this way: "An all night disc jockey, good with gab, started talking more and more, and was playing less and less music. Finally, he ignored the stack of records he was supposed to play. His audience grew. Voila! Talk Radio." But one thing we do know. Rush Limbaugh made it popular – and profitable. Rush doesn't stray far off politics, and his audience likes it that way. The Republicans swear they don't subsidize his show. Conservative Talk Radio continues to grow in stations and listeners. As a counter move, the Liberals have started up their own talk shows. But they don't have the pizazz, as Rush's program does. (Rush is America's most popular talk show host, and is heard on 600 stations.)

When it comes to politics, WCCO isn't biased one way or another. But many of its callers and texters are. They're not bashful about stating their side of an issue. Not all are open-minded; many refuse to listen to the other side. And they love to get in on some good old fashioned, smash-mouth discussions on just about everything: politics, taxes, rapists, school issues, Obamacare, child abuse, teenage sex, discrimination, entertainment, the international crisis, Black Friday, low wages, Ebola virus, gas prices, the Vikings – and you name it. All these subjects have been touched on recently, with one or more of the WCCO talk show hosts: John Hines, Chad Hartman, John Williams, Jordana Green, Al Malmberg, and Jon Grayson, WCCO's overnight announcer.

Talk Radio is good at problem solving. Feeling fatigued? Is Creeping Charlie killing your lawn? Have an embarrassing weather-faded deck? Know the basic steps in getting your house ready for sale? Is that 2008 Buick Lacrosse running rough? Disappointed with your financial portfolio? Humming birds not coming to their feeder? WCCO's Denny Long tackles these, and similar kinds of problems, every weekend. His scads of programs address medical issues, lawn and garden, home improvement, real estate, car care, financial advice, and nature notes. Each show features one or more experts in their field; trying hard to find the right solution for the caller or texter. I'm sure the listening audience does like I do, and stores away the information learned for future reference.

Having been a fan of Denny's for more years than I can remember, I call him, "the weekend wonder." How he produces all those programs, is beyond me. Something I like about him, he's genuinely interested in the listener's problem, and never tries to upstage the host or experts. One popular program, *Healthy Matters*, airs Sunday mornings, 7:30–8:30 a.m., and features Dr. David Hilden, MD Department, Internal Medicine, Hennepin County Medical Center, downtown Minneapolis. As host, Dr. Hilden covers everything from headaches to heart attacks. With him are medical experts in their specific field of medicine. The program exemplifies the valuable service that WCCO offers its listeners.

Morning Lee-dership
The Twin Cities rise and shine with Dave Lee

Dave Lee has the morning radio drive-time slot – 5-9:00 a.m. – when most home and car radios are on. A wide-awake kind of guy, Dave Lee fits the part perfectly, as the host of *The WCCO Morning News With Dave Lee*. His show has all the elements for today's fast-paced, or crazy busy, lifestyle. I compare him to a circus ringmaster, as he presents all the acts at the precise time: news, weather, road conditions, sports reports, entertainment, and newsmakers from every field. He has been nominated as one of the Top Five major market hosts nationwide. He personally has won countless broadcasting awards to keep WCCO's trophy wall, overflowing. An avid sports guy, Dave has done color for Twins games, and is doing the University of St. Thomas football play-by-play. For a morning bonus, listeners are enjoying "Extra Innings," from time to time, with Dave Lee, and John Hines, at 9:10 a.m.

Dave Lee may be eligible for a page in the Guinness World Records. He is the only living soul to turn WCCO Radio down for an announcing job offer. This was in the 1980s, when Dave worked at KFGO 790 AM, Fargo, North Dakota. He was a happy camper, and saw no need to move to the larger Twin Cities' market. Then, in 1989, WCCO called again. This time Dave was ready for Minnesota's Good Neighbor Station. And his fans are sure glad he agreed to cross the border to WCCO Radio.

With his farm background, getting up with the chickens to be on the air at 5:00 a.m., is no problem for Dave. Growing up in Hatton, North Dakota, farm kids were expected to rise and shine at the crack of dawn. Continuing the habit has earned Dave some kudos. The program is an industry award winner. Also, it's a big winner with his morning audience. ∎

-8-

THE INFORMATION AGE

Dedicated to News

WCCO's main entrée is served all day

We've become news junkies. Even with the media's countless sources, the public never seems to get its fill. That's one of the reasons WCCO Radio wisely reinvented itself into a news/talk format station, a number of years ago. Their goal was to expand the news scene, and satisfy the listener's insatiable appetite for information. And they've got the people and facilities to do it. You should see the WCCO newsroom. It's the heart of the station, and the envy of the industry. Sig Mickelson and Jim Bormann, news directors, raised the bar for news operations in the 1950s, and the industry has never taken its eyes off WCCO since.

Today, WCCO's newsroom is still the busiest spot in the station, and abounds with the latest in technology. While one news reporter is on their cell phone checking facts for their next newscast, another is finishing a story on a laptop. When I was there in 1950, it was still those loud, clacking typewriters that always needed a ribbon change. And today's hi-tech AP teletype machines are a whole lot quieter, with no more paper jams, as they transmit reports from all over the world, using the internet. But something that hasn't changed – WCCO's high journalistic standards. To meet the tight deadlines, it takes good writing skills and discipline, something the news staff also has plenty of.

The Newsmakers
WCCO stays close to those who make the news

WCCO has always had an uncanny ability to scoop the competition by getting first to the newsmakers in all fields: politics, the public sector, sports, business, medicine, education, science, technology, real estate, and entertainment. Perhaps the epitome of newsmakers was Hubert H. Humphrey. He made news in every office he held. First, as the mayor of Minneapolis, then as a Minnesota U.S. Senator. Next, Vice President, under Lyndon Johnson. As V.P., he told his staff in Washington, D.C.: "If those folks from WCCO Radio, phone, put the call right through."

When Humphrey came home to visit constituents, he often stopped off at the station to say "hello," and give an interview. Minnesota's Walter Mondale, a U.S. Senator, and Vice President under Jimmy Carter in 1977 – and Humphrey's protégé – is also a good friend of WCCO. Even as elder statesmen, they both continued their close ties with the station. That's the kind of credibility WCCO has among newsmakers. The station has earned the reputation for being the most trusted source for news and information in Minnesota.

Listening to today's news staff, including Steve Simpson, Daphne Adato, Edgar Linares, Laura Oakes, Al Schoch, and Susie Jones – tells you that a news career is right up their alley. They all have a nose for news, the first requirement for being a good newsperson. Their on-air presence is professional and authoritative. Students studying their five "W's" – who, what, when, where, and why, at the journalism schools at the Universities of Minnesota and Missouri, would love a news position at WCCO Radio. Would they give their first born to win it? Okay, no. But I bet they'd be willing to become a mentor, and help others pursuing a broadcast journalism career.

Top 25 News Stories
Lots of history spanning 90 years

When WCCO Radio first signed on in 1924, there was no official news department. That came later, during World War II. And since the station had no history of what constituted radio news, the announcer on duty, oblivious to copyright laws, would read stories right from the *Minneapolis Journal,* that happened to be handy. And who knows. Had an official from the *Journal* heard the broadcast – heard the news from right off their front page – they may have been in more of a complimentary mood than a lawsuit mood.

WCCO has changed a lot since then, and prides itself on having one of the finest news departments in the country. Here is just a handful of the headlines from among the thousands of stories they've broadcast. You'll see that they represent all categories of news – local, regional, national, and international:

- **WCCO brings radio to the region** – October 1, 1924
- **WPA puts unemployed to work**- 1935
- **Armistice Day blizzard shocks hunters** – November 11, 1940
- **Gopher's Bruce Smith wins Heisman Trophy** – 1941
- **Japan bombs Pearl Harbor** – December 7, 1941
- **Peace! World War II ends**- September 2, 1945
- **Twin Cities now "Major League" with Twins & Vikings** – 1961
- **Cedric Adams – Minnesota's favorite broadcaster – dies** – 1961
- **John F. Kennedy assassinated** – November 22, 1963
- **Hubert Humphrey nominated for Vice President** – 1964
- **America's first on the moon** – July 20, 1969
- **Herb Brooks upsets Russian Olympic hockey team** – 1980
- **Twins win World Series** – 1987
- **Mikhail Gorbachev visits Twin Cities** – 1990
- **Halloween blizzard scares Minnesota** – October 31, 1991
- **Minnesota's coldest day; minus 60 in Tower** – 1993
- **Terrorists attack Twin Towers** – September 11, 2001
- **Senator Paul Wellstone dies in plane crash** – 2002
- **35W Bridge collapses; kills 13** – 2007
- **Franken ousts Coleman by 225 votes** – 2009
- **Amy Senser charged in I-94 ramp death** – 2011
- **Obama re-elected to 2nd term** – 2012
- **Adrian Peterson charged with whipping son** – 2014
- **Ebola virus spreads to America** – 2014
- **Gov. Dayton wins 2nd term** – 2014

Here's a news challenge for you. Take a moment to check the number of above stories you're familiar with. If you scored 15 or more points, you're a "history major." Congratulations!

Weather Watch
WCCO meteorologists keep an eye on the sky

Weather is always on our mind in Minnesota. That's why WCCO Radio treats the weather only one way – seriously. When weather warnings occur, lots of new, or part time listeners tune in, as they know 'CCO is the best source for severe weather conditions, be it a tornado, snowstorm, hail, flash flood warning, or an extreme arctic cold blast. The station is fortunate to have Mike Lynch, a crackerjack of a meteorologist. He knows his stuff. His morning reports with Dave Lee, and all through the morning, are enlightening and thorough. And when that troubling weather does pop up, so does Mike, with the tracking story. I remember him following a special story about Tower, a tiny town in northeast Minnesota. Their thermometer on February 2, 1993, officially reached minus 60 degrees F., for Minnesota's coldest temperature, ever. Governor Arne Carlson closed all Minnesota schools that same day. (It was minus 32 degrees in Minneapolis/St. Paul.) Mike Lynch had a lot to talk about on that cold, and bitter day. It's another weather milestone he has covered for his thousands of listeners on WCCO.

During winter, school kids remember it's 8-3-0 on the dial that tells them if their school is going to be a "lucky one," among the closing announcements. Because it's "official," when it's heard on WCCO Radio.   ■

-9-

LIFE AFTER WCCO

Paying Your Dues

Small town stations feature first time announcers

My pageboy experience was a big stepping stone for me. It led to an exciting 35-year broadcasting and advertising career. My next stop, after leaving WCCO in 1951, was an announcing job in Eau Claire, Wisconsin. It was quite a culture shock going from a powerful 50,000 watt clear channel station, to a small town 250 watt radio station. But it was all part of paying your dues. That's what hundreds of young announcers were doing all across the country. Me included. Radio school gave us the skills for that first level position. And we were eager to succeed, in order to advance our careers.

WBIZ Radio served a college town of 35,000. (Now, population 67,000.) It was located in west-central Wisconsin, the heart of America's dairy country, and the home of the University of Wisconsin, Eau Claire. WBIZ AM 1400 was a 250-watt station, an affiliate of the Mutual Broadcasting System. After sending them an audition tape, I was hired. Forty dollars a week was my starting salary. Peanuts? Maybe. But that $40.00 had plenty of purchasing power in 1951. A nickel bought a cup of coffee, a Milky Way, or a Pepsi Cola. Regular gasoline was 29.9 cents a gallon. And a nice two-bedroom home cost a little under $7,500.

I barely got through the front door when Stan Torgelson, manager, rushed me to a one-hour remote broadcast at the Northern Wisconsin Fair in Chippewa Falls, a neighboring town. (What? No week's training orientation?) I felt right at home interviewing fairgoers, as I had done at the WCCO Radio booth at the Minnesota State Fair, the year before. For my first on-air job, I guess I passed the test, as Stan seemed happy with my performance. He soon gave me similar assignments, including the color broadcast job for high school basketball games.

My WBIZ colleagues went out of their way to show me the ropes. There was Stan Torgelson, Jerry Thomas, Lou Kassera, Bob Benson, and the station owner, Howard Bill. I had the late shift from 4:00 p.m. to sign-off at midnight. Besides operating the studio control board, which took several days to master, I was a staff announcer, disc jockey, newscaster, sports color announcer, and dabbled in radio sales.

As a Mutual affiliate, we carried all those great radio dramas and mysteries that the network was famous for – i.e., *The Shadow, I Love A Mystery, The Green Hornet, The Lone Ranger, Wild Bill Hickok,* and *The Adventures of Superman.* Not many knew it, but Mutual, unlike ABC, CBS and NBC, operated as a cooperative until 1952. They touted more affiliates than any other network.

While still at WBIZ, my draft papers came in November 1951. The Korean War was expanding, and the UN needed more ground troops. I thought I was going in the army, but the U.S. Marine Corps was drafting, also, and I was headed for boot camp in San Diego. Next came combat training at Camp Pendleton; then an upper bunk on the USS Walker troop ship, aimed for Korea. The Marines are pretty good at putting you where you're needed. They assigned me to P.I.O. (Public Information Office, now Public Affairs), and made me a radio correspondent, which fit nicely in my plans for a broadcasting career.

Marine Radio Correspondent
Minneapolis Marine scores Ted Williams interview

I crossed paths several times with Ted Williams, the baseball Hall of Famer. First, as an eight-year old kid, watching him play Triple-A baseball with the Minneapolis Millers. Then, 15-years later, we met during the Korean War when I was a Marine Radio Correspondent. He was on the USS Haven, a

United Nations hospital ship, just off the coast of Pusan in eastern Korea. He was convalescing from a touch of pneumonia. Williams was a U.S. Marine reservist, and was recalled for duty in Korea, which interrupted his baseball career. As a Marine jet fighter pilot, Capt. Ted Williams wanted to do his job, and be left alone from the media. He shunned the reporters, as he had in Boston playing for the Red Sox. So I knew that interviewing him was not a given, but worth a gung-ho try.

By dinghy, I went out to the hospital ship on April 13, 1953, to meet one of baseball's greatest hitters. A Navy Corpsman escorted me to the social hall, where Williams was resting and wearing a hospital robe. As I sensed a good story, my mind wondered back to Nicollet Park when he played for the Minneapolis Millers, in 1938. He was tall, lanky, and 20, while I was only eight, and a member of the Knothole Gang. We got in the game free. For a nickel you could have a cold Nesbitt's Orange Soda. Another nickel bought you a big bag of peanuts. Boy, that was bleacher heaven! Ted Williams was my hero on Saturdays when I saw him play with the Millers. Now, here he was 15-years later, in Korea, playing a more dangerous kind of game with his Marine Corps Panther jet.

I introduced myself and requested a tape interview for *The Marine Corps Show*. He politely turned me down. I tried to hide my disappointment. But I wasn't going to be denied. I had lugged all my heavy recording equipment this far, and I wasn't going back without a story. I thought about his days in Minneapolis, and then spoke. "Capt. Williams, I used to watch you play for the Millers," I said, hoping it would hit his hot button.

His mood changed a little. "You did, sergeant? What year was that?" he asked.

"It would have been 1938, because you went to the Red Sox in1939," I answered.

"What position did I play?" he asked, further testing me.

He nearly had me. I had to recall the outfield spot where I saw him. I knew it was left field in Boston. "Right field," I tried.

"What was the name of the ball park," he came back with, almost hoping I wouldn't know.

That was easy. Everyone from Minneapolis knew about Nicollet Park at Lake Street and Nicollet Avenue. I told him, and he nodded to confirm I was right.

He quizzed me again: "What was my number?"

I had to think about that one. I knew it was number nine with the Red Sox. It probably was the same for his farm team. But wait. Was this a trap? Maybe he wore a different number with the Millers. Then it hit me. I was a kid again sitting there in the bleachers. I could see Ted Williams, plain as day, with number nine on the back of his uniform. "Nine," I almost shouted.

"OK, wise guy. How many homers did I hit that year?"

I was only eight years old at the time, but pretty good with baseball stats. "How many homers? Forty," I shot back.

"Wrong," he said, and corrected me. "It was 43." He sounded proud of his batting achievement, as it won him the Triple Crown in the American Association.

Williams was pretty good with stats, too. And he could sure play hardball with all his questions. Then he smiled his famous Ted Williams smile, and laughed. He agreed to the tape interview. I quickly got my Webcor tape recorder ready, turned it on, tested it, and introduced Capt. Ted Williams on the tape. I asked about his narrow escape when he crash-landed his Panther jet after being hit by ground fire. And we talked plenty of baseball, like his grand slammer in Detroit during the 1941 All Star game. (To win the game.) And who was going to win the upcoming 1953 World Series? He predicted the Yankees would beat the Brooklyn Dodgers – which they did, six months later. I also asked about his future plans – after Korea – and he said it was up to the Red Sox. But he felt he had a few more good years in him. He was 35 at the time, and did return to baseball for several years.

I didn't realize how big the story was until I got back to PIO headquarters, by the 38th parallel. Capt Bem Price, PIO Officer, heard the tape twice, and said, "You've got an exclusive," Sergeant Hill. "And you broke Williams' media silence. This is probably the biggest interview in the Korean War. Nice going."

The story went over the wire worldwide on AP, and was broadcast on all the radio networks – ABC, CBS, Mutual, NBC – and on the *Marine Corps Radio Show* on NBC. Down on the rest of the media, it was the only interview Ted Williams gave while serving in Korea. He consented, because we had a special connection. I had seen him play with the Minneapolis Millers when I was eight years old.

Campbell Mithun Advertising
A paunchy TV bear put them on the map

In the mid-1950s, Campbell Mithun was one of the hot shops. Their Hamm's Beer TV campaign – "From the Land of Sky Blue Waters" – was the talk of the industry. I joined them in 1957. I was out of the Marines, married, and working in Minneapolis at Channel 9, KEYD-TV, in the Foshay Tower. (Now KMSP-TV in Eden Prairie, Minnesota.) A friend from Campbell Mithun, Art Lund, a radio/TV producer, mentioned that C-M had just landed the Kroger Food Store account, and was hiring. He knew I was interested in an ad agency job. So, during my lunch hour I hightailed over to their 13th floor offices in the Northwestern National Bank Building. They needed radio/TV writers – like now. I had the qualifications and was hired. But there was just one hitch. The entire account was moving to C-M's Chicago office. Talking it over with Mary, my wife, she said: "Let's go for it." It would turn out to be the right decision and a real adventure for us. We ended up spending 12 years there, living in Northbrook, 30-miles north of Chicago, one of Chicago's hundreds of bedroom communities.

Worth noting were the hours. In Minneapolis, we started at 8:30 a.m. In Chicago, 9:00 a.m. (Which seemed like the middle of the day.) But habits are hard to break. So most of us who transferred to the Chicago C-M office, showed up earlier. Jim Smith, my boss on the Kroger account, would come in around 6:00 a.m. (To avoid traffic, and get away early to play golf.) Jim, with his General Mills experience with Gold Medal Flour, was the guy with plenty of good marketing ideas. He would get numerous calls from the Minneapolis office asking his advice. Jim would steer them right. Especially, regarding retail problems.

With my announcing background, I became the resident in-house announcer for Campbell Mithun. This entailed mostly radio and TV test-commercials for the Chicago office accounts, including: American Dairy Association, Helene Curtis, Kroger, Wilson Sporting Goods, and others. It was a nice change of pace from routine office duties. The agency had a state of the art production studio to work with. Jack Maribelli was the production engineer, and knew his business. On lucky days, more times than not, I would record a spot on the first take. Jack tallied up the commercials and presentation tapes, which was well over 1,000 during my 12 years in the Chicago office.

After six months, I moved from copywriting into producing radio/TV commercials for Kroger's network of 350 radio and 65 TV stations. One project was the *Mickey Mouse Club* that Walt Disney produced for television. It was the most popular kid show in the 1950s. I spent two days in the Disney Burbank, California studios, picking footage of Mickey and his pals, for Kroger commercials. (It was the first time Disney allowed outsiders inside his movie vaults.) Disney also made Jimmie Dodd, head Mouseketeer, available for merchandising purposes. We used him in commercials and for personal appearances at Kroger stores. I got to know him fairly well, and had remembered him for his bit parts in movies, including *Flying Tigers* with John Wayne. He was older than he looked. That's why Disney suggested a turtle neck sweater for his costume — to hide any wrinkles. Also, the studio insisted that James Dodd go by "Jimmie," which in and of itself, appeared to make him "look" years younger. Incidentally, it was Dodd who wrote the M-I-C-K-E-Y M-O-U-S-E song that every kid in America loved to sing. The *Mickey Mouse Club* won the rating game in every Kroger market it ran. Needless to say, Kroger was a very happy client, as store sales exceeded their sales forecast.

Another Campbell Mithun account celebrating their bottom line, was Hamm's Beer. Barrelage was at an all time high for the St. Paul brewery, thanks to expansion. They were having good success at opening new markets in Baltimore, Dallas, Huston, and San Francisco. But they hit the proverbial wall in Chicago. The sales people heard nothing but "No," when they made cold calls on Chicagoland taverns in the late 1950's. "See all those beer signs," one manager said. "I carry 26 kinds — domestic and imported. Not counting the tap beer. Why would I want another brand of beer?"

Hamm's management was almost ready to write off Chicago when Ray Mithun, co-founder of Campbell Mithun, heard about it. He suggested using "forced distribution." The plan was to run the "Land of Sky Blue Waters" television commercials to create consumer demand. Did it work? Almost immediately after the Hamm's paunchy cartoon bear hit the TV screens, hard working Chicagoans, in their favorite taverns, asked for the beer that,

that funny bear sells. Mithun's marketing tool unlocked the sales logjam. Customers "forced" the tavern owners to stock Hamm's Beer. Pretty soon the Budweiser, Miller, Pabst Blue Ribbon, Blatz, Leinenkugel's, and Schlitz signs, all had company. In came the Hamm's Beer point of purchase material – clocks, signs and displays. (Signage and P.O.P. in the brewery industry, is the biggest advertising expense; more than the million dollar media budgets.)

There are many versions of how the Hamm's animated TV bear mascot came to be. I can give you the real McCoy story, which I stumbled on. During an agency dinner in Chicago, I sat next to Alden Grimes, account supervisor on the American Dairy Association account. As the former research director of Campbell Mithun in Minneapolis, he was directly involved in the development of most of the agency campaigns. While making small talk, I asked about his most exciting moment in advertising. Without batting an eye he said, "Land of Sky Blue Waters." I asked him who came up with the bear idea. That's when he got excited, and told me the whole story how the campaign evolved. These were his words that he later was kind enough to put in a memo, as he knew I was keenly interested in the campaign:

> *"In the early 1950's, the Theo. Hamm Brewing Company, a client of ours, was looking to replace their current theme, 'The Gold Standard of Beer.' Assigned to the project was Don Grawert, copywriter, and Cleo Hovel, art director. (No ordinary artist, Hovel had valuable Walt Disney experience.) Starting on the project, Grawert remembered a line he had seen in a Land O'Lakes Butter newspaper ad: 'The Land of Sky Blue Waters.' (The phrase is from a Henry Wadsworth Longfellow poem, 'The Song of Hiawatha.') Grawert walked two offices away to see the writer, since Land O'Lakes was also a Campbell Mithun client. Told he had no future plans for the line, Grawert met with Cleo Hovel. Both agreed that the phrase, 'From the Land of Sky Blue Waters,' had some scratch, or potential. They immediately went to work on the project.*
>
> *A week later Grawert and Hovel were ready to bounce off their new Hamm's Beer concept on me. As I entered Cleo's office I noticed 20 or so rough sketches and TV storyboards on all four walls, and even some on the floor. The layouts were grabbers. I couldn't take my eyes off them.*

Hovel had developed a paunchy looking cartoon bear in numerous poses; by pine trees, by blue water and with lots of critters surrounding the bear in a north woods setting. In some layouts he was smiling; others, embarrassed. In all the sketches, the little guy oozed with personality. You could feel something special in the room. Grawert and Hovel were trying to hide their excitement, as they wanted to see my reaction first. I nearly peed in my pants. The layouts were that compelling. It took an artist of Cleo Hovel's genius to develop the idea and execute it. And it was to become one of advertising's most classic campaigns for both print and television."

Alden Grimes

For a project the scope of "The Land of Sky Blue Waters," Campbell Mithun used a ton of outside suppliers in 1952 (i.e., Art designers, printers, recording and film studios, and musicians). For the music, the agency recruited Ernie Garvin, a WCCO Radio musician and singer. Garvin created the now famous jingle, with the tom-tom beat. Vocalists on the soundtrack, besides Ernie, included his brother, Hal, Burt Hanson, and Dick Link, all mainstay musicians with WCCO. (See page 57 for their photos.)

Minneapolis – New Ad Center
Ray Mithun's creative crusade paid off

There was a time when it seemed like national advertisers were discriminating against smaller market ad agencies. (The 1940s and early 1950s.) No collusion was involved, so there wasn't a legal issue. Campbell Mithun, headquartered in Minneapolis – the 15th largest market – was one of those agencies affected. Old school thinking was that only Madison Avenue in New York City, could produce "the big idea." Could it be that some ad managers wanted an ad agency in the Big Apple so they could be "royally wined and dined?" I certainly hope not. Eventually, Chicago's advertising style was accepted, thanks to Leo Burnett, founder of the Leo Burnett Agency. (He had Kellogg's, Campbell Soup, and Marlboro.) But New York was still getting most of the blue chip accounts.

Ray Mithun fought this misguided myth for years. He was out to show national advertisers that Minneapolis was a productive creative center. Ray's crusade paid off. In the late 1950s, and early 1960s, Campbell Mithun was regarded within the industry as a hot shop. The "Land of Sky Blue Waters" campaign for Hamm's Beer, and other creative work, was called refreshing. With Campbell Mithun leading the charge, Minneapolis was recognized as a top creative hub. Other shops contributing to Minneapolis' advertising growth, included: Fallon McElligot & Rice, Carmichael Lynch, Knox Reeves, Colle McVoy, Martin Williams, and Bolin.

Campbell Mithun Loses Hamm's
...and consumers lose their funny bear

If you're in the ad agency business, as sure as night follows day, you're going to lose some accounts. It could be when you least expect it, or maybe through no fault of your own. Those five little words: "...no longer agency of record," are hard to swallow. One main reason for switching agencies is due to a change on the client side. A new advertising director may want to start a new agency relationship. When Ray Mithun received "the call," from the Theo. Hamm Brewing Company, he learned that J. Walter Thompson in Chicago, was the new advertising agency. The reason given for the change was that the new agency had worldwide merchandising capabilities. Excuse me for editorializing, but phooey! Campbell Mithun, since its inception in 1933, was a *pioneer* in merchandising. Ray Mithun was personally involved in the one-pound packages of Land O'Lakes Butter. In the 1930s butter was sold bulk, and sent home on waxed butcher paper. Those neat, eye-catching cartons changed all that. Land O'Lakes soon became the #1 butter brand in America. (See photo on page 63.)

Bob Pile, account supervisor on the Hamm's account, would have had every right to meet with his former client, and say: *"Look, didn't we create a new ad campaign for you that met your goals? Didn't we help you expand to new markets to achieve record barrelage? Didn't you yourself recently say your profits skyrocketed? Now, what's this sh__ – I mean – what's this sh-enanigan about changing agencies?"* Bob Pile, who directed the Hamm's classic advertising campaign, could have said all that. But like the professional he was, he didn't. One reason was because Pile knew that the client would use the old classical client retort: "Sure, you've done all that – but what have you done for me lately?"

Something Ray Mithun did was unprecedented. Rather than sending the traditional "goodbye letter" – thanking the client for all the good times – he produced a ten minute video tape for Hamm's management. He didn't plead, or beg, to have Hamm's change their mind about the agency's dismissal. The purpose was to have the St. Paul brewery stay the course. In essence it said: *"Look. We know you fired us. And we accept that. But please think twice if you're considering a new creative direction. Your Hamm's bear mascot, and 'Land of Sky Blue Waters,' theme, are too valuable to abandon. You've poured millions of advertising dollars into the campaign – and your huge increase in barrelage proves it's working. Stay the course."*

What was the first thing Hamm's and J. Walter Thompson did? They scrapped the campaign, as Ray Mithun suspected they would. The new TV commercials used a real live bear and an outdoor woodsman dressed like Paul Bunyan. Sales went south so fast that even Ray Mithun, who had every reason to gloat, felt sorry for them. It was the beginning of the end for Hamm's Beer. Today, MillerCoors owns the brand, and does very little Hamm's advertising. You have to look hard to find a can of that once famous beer, with that paunchy, funny, cartoon bear. Once, one of TV's favorite icons.

So, mamas, don't let your babies grow up to join an ad agency. The heartbreak can be too much if a client pulls the plug. Especially when the agency switch is zero-productive. Sorry to say, but sometimes egos can get in the way of sound business decisions. In the case of Hamm's, it was the consumer who had the last word.

The New Mithun

The agency's compass is pointed toward – "success!"

With new facilities in the historic 510 Marquette Building to inspire them, and Ray Mithun's spirit to guide them, and a new identity to instill new pride, the agency team at Mithun is ready for today's challenges. Campbell Mithun – now renamed Mithun – is well respected in the industry. Started in 1933, during the darkest days of the Great Depression, the founders, Ralph Campbell and Ray Mithun, left a solid foundation that today's staff can proudly build on. Such as Ray Mithun being inducted into Advertising's prestigious Hall of Fame in 1989. Known for great advertising, the agency continues the tradition under new leadership. Rob Buchner, formerly with

Minneapolis' Fallon, is CEO. David Carter is the creative officer. Both are experienced leaders with their eye on the ball.

With unlimited choices, media decisions are more critical than ever. That's why more and more advertisers are choosing Mithun's Compass Point Media, a full service media agency. It has 100 top media professionals managing $600M+. To show the agency's further strength, Mithun is part of Interpublic Group of Communications Company, a global leader in modern marketing solutions.

The Mithun agency continues to add some nice business to existing accounts. Here's just a snippet of their clients: Wellmark Blue Cross Blue Shield, Toro, General Mills, Green Giant, and Johnsonville Foods. Also, Chipotle, Ashley Furniture, Pandora, Key Bank, Popeyes, Workday, and Land O'Lakes, a client the agency has served for 80+ years.

The Wrap-Up
Lessons learned from two special companies

Both companies are in communications. Both are pioneers and leaders in their respective fields. Both are headquartered in Minneapolis. And they're joined together with an ongoing business relationship of 80+ years. My career highlight is having worked at both organizations – WCCO Radio and Campbell Mithun. It was like their staffs were interchangeable. People at both places have a bias for action, and are loaded with talent and confidence. Both companies have trophy walls that dazzle the eye. A sure sign they're doing something right.

It wasn't but a few days after I joined WCCO when I felt the drive for excellence. And we pageboys weren't left out. I was taught to never be satisfied with the status quo. Instead, to "reach for the stars." Pretty heady stuff for a teenager, but the message got through.

I'm delighted to see Ray Mithun's principles still being used at the new Mithun Agency. They are as sound today, as they were nearly 60 years ago, when I followed this sage advice in the Chicago office's landmark Palmolive Building, on Michigan Avenue:

**"There is only one reason for the existence of this business.
To help our clients solve their problems."**

-Ray Mithun

Another lesson learned is from Ray Mithun's "Everything Talks," memo. Beyond advertising, the agency believes in total marketing, as Mithun explains:

> **"We had better try to help in every part of the communications job, because everything talks:**
> **The product design.**
> **The packaging.**
> **The communications form.**
> **Not just the advertising."**

-Ray Mithun

This last principle has led to some groundbreaking advertising, including the Hamm's Beer classic campaign – "From the Land of Sky Blue Waters":

> **"Which way is North?**
> **To create great advertising, we need**
> **to be headed in the right direction."**

-Ray Mithun

■

Photo Index

CPSIA information can be obtained at www.ICGtesting.com
Printed in the USA
LVOW04s1535140815

450133LV00005B/8/P